HASH HOUSE HARRIERS ON YOU!

© Copyright M. C. Williams January 2006-March 2008

All rights reserved. Printed in the United Kingdom and/or the USA. No part of this publication may be reproduced, stored in a retrieval system, or transmitted, in any form or by any means, electronic, mechanical, photocopying, recording, or otherwise, without the prior written permission of the publisher and/or the author; except in the case of reviewers who may quote brief passages in a review.

Hash House Harriers - On You!
ISBN-13: 978-1-9066280-1-7

Published by CheckPoint Press, Ireland

CHECKPOINT PRESS, DOOAGH, ACHILL ISLAND, CO. MAYO, REPUBLIC OF IRELAND
TEL: 098 43779   INTERNATIONAL: 00353 9843779
WWW.CHECKPOINTPRESS.COM
EMAIL: EDITOR@CHECKPOINTPRESS.COM

Hash House Harriers On You!

ACKNOWLEDGEMENTS

The events portrayed in this book are true. If any hashers remember things differently, one of us must have had too much to drink! I would like to thank everyone who has contributed to the text knowingly, or unknowingly, and I particularly want to say a big thank you to the Isle of Wight hash for making my time with them so memorable.

Thanks also to Fracas and Di for proof reading.

I am now leaving the Isle of Wight to work in Birmingham - that well known hashing desert. I will try some missionary work and see if I can convince the Brummies to get into the hashing spirit.

All I can really say is 'ON ON'.

Navigator

N.B. Some names have been changed to protect the innocent.

CONTENTS

Chapter 1
This is Hashing on the Isle of Wight   page 9

Chapter 2
Corfe Farm Run   page 17

Chapter 3
Yorkshire - Queen's Golden Jubilee Hash   page 23

Chapter 4
Holmfirth   page 33

Chapter 5
Carisbrook Castle Run   page 37

Chapter 6
Cherbourg   page 39

Chapter 7
Alverstone Run   page 49

Chapter 8
Eurohash Aarhus   page 53

Chapter 9
Nash Hash in the Cotswolds   page 69

Chapter 10
The Isle of Wight Thousandth Run   page 77

Chapter 11
And Then there was Essex   page 85

Chapter 12
Interhash 2004 Cardiff   page 91

Chapter 13
Havenstreet Station Run   page 103

Chapter 14
Seaview Dog Day Run   page 109

Chapter 15
Eurohash 2005 Amsterdam   page 115

Chapter 1

This is Hashing on the Isle of Wight

The view from near the summit of Clatterford Hill on the Isle of Wight is spectacular. To the east is Carisbrook Castle a huge stone monolith guarding the island's capital, Newport. To the west, a line of perfectly rounded hills marches down to the horizon, the shadows of clouds gradually drifting across them. To the North is the Solent and a clear view across to Portsmouth and Southampton Water; white sails billowing in the wind on hundreds of small sailing craft. The only blot on the landscape is the oil refinery at Fawley; black smoke staining the sky, spoiling what is otherwise an idyllic scene.

I actually have very little time to take this all in, as I am attempting to run up to the top of the hill as quickly as possible. It is eleven thirty on Sunday morning and I consider, not for the first time, what I am doing here. I could have stayed in bed with my wife, watched the television, read the newspapers and convinced one of my children to make me a cup of tea. But, no, I had travelled the seven miles from Ryde to Newport just to follow a trail of white flour over a five-mile course; the blobs of flour are leading up what feels like a vertical incline. I am trying to convince my legs to move and losing the argument!

This is hashing! There are about thirty of us, all climbing the hill and looking for flour. The Hash House Harriers is called by some the drinking club with a running problem. This is not far from the truth! Every Sunday a group of us get together to follow a trail laid out the day before by a fellow hasher known as a hare. The trail starts at a pub and finishes back at the same pub.

Three white blobs in a row mean the trail goes in this direction; a call of 'On! On!' indicates the trail has been found. A circle indicates a check; these are located at junctions and mean that all of the directions should be checked out until three blobs of flour are found. A call of 'On You!' means 'does the trail go this way?'

I leave checking activities to those fit members of the Hash who can actually run rather than trot, as if you get the direction wrong you will have to run back and catch up with everyone else. There are also fishhooks (flour laid in the shape of a hook on the trail) that require the first five or so runners who reach them to turn round and run to the back of the pack. This is a good idea as it slows down the fit ones, preventing them from getting too far ahead. There are also line outs - white lines of flour that are not to be crossed under any circumstances.

Excellent news! The path at the top of the hill is 'lined out': all those runners in front of me are making their way back down the hill. I am now third from the front rather than trailing at the back. I will make the most of this, putting on a downhill spurt and keeping well ahead. A nice idea, but Shergar* has just passed me - he clearly has good form on the downhill dry sections. Stalker is also closing in; he is a proper runner who takes marathons in his stride. Disaster! A fish hook I am fifth in line - I should really go back behind the rest of the pack and then run on, I will try and avoid this by pretending I have missed it. I am sure no one will notice, as I am not usually the type to get involved in fishhooks.

I seem to have got away with the fishhook. No one is paying me any attention; it is all downhill now and very easy going. I can hear the gentle babbling of a stream ahead. The trees are forming a canopy

---

Hashers generally have a hash handle (nick name by which they are known to other hashers). Hash members give these names to each other, usually in response to some misdemeanour.

Shergar is an Irish guy who runs like a horse, he also got lost (went missing) on his first ever run. I am called Navigator because of my inability to find anywhere. Some others are known as Fat Bastard, Miss Whiplash, and Shit for Brains(never has a name been more apt!).

1: This is Hashing on the Isle of Wight

over the path and the ground is dappled with sunlight. This running is pretty good; everything is fine with the world.

Oh, No! There is a ford in the road and the bridge for pedestrians is 'lined out'. In the middle of the water is Hard On (don't ask!) who enjoys baptising people I am not talking about a few splashes either. He seems to be of the Baptist persuasion - only full immersion will do. Hard On is at least six foot two inches and weighs about nineteen stone. He seems to be involved in an attempt to drown Dangerous, a large, bald cockney who used to know gangsters in the East End of London (hence the name Dangerous). I will sneak through while they are occupied.

I am now very wet - Dangerous and Hard On united against the sneaky Navigator who evaded a fishhook earlier on. The water was fairly cold but I did not go under without a fight! At least they are both soaked as well! The trail is now heading uphill towards Carisbrook Castle. I feel a short cut coming on. Hard On is joining me and we are dripping our way back towards the pub and the cars. A quick change of clothes and we are ready for a few beers.

The Waverly pub (named after a paddle steamer that used to travel between Southampton and Cowes) is situated at the top of the High Street Carisbrook and is basically a Victorian building that had a makeover in the early 60s: the windows are small and rectangular; cream coloured window frames are spaced regularly in a two storey brick box. There is a good-sized car park and a peeling sign showing the paddle steamer in all her former glory.

Inside, the 60s theme continues, with two separate bars, one used for dining. The tables no longer have Formica tops but they could quickly revert if given a chance! A narrow passage leads to a small door and you eventually arrive in the drinking bar. This is furnished with a few seats around the edge and just two small tables.

This room is given over to standing at the bar and drinking - none of your namby pamby comfortable chairs and areas to relax, just hard stools and a bell to pull if you want your pint topping up. Here you can drink yourself into temporal oblivion, listening to the Beatles, Rolling Stones and Cilla Black on the juke box. The landlord is welcoming and the beer is excellent.

The hash all head for the drinking bar. There is a certain inverted snobbery in hash circles: we don't do foody pubs where you sit down to enjoy a pint and are immediately asked whether you will you be eating now or later? Well sometimes we do, but the response is usually 'Will you please go away! (Something like that anyway, but often involving the word off) we want to have a quiet drink. It says "PUBLIC HOUSE" on the sign outside, not "RESTAURANT"! If it had said "restaurant" we would not have come in. Will you please leave us alone. If we want to eat we will tell you.'

The tradition after a run is to have some 'down downs'. These involve drinking a pint of beer in one go while the rest of the hash sing a song. The beer glass must not be removed from the lips until finished. Then the empty glass should be inverted and placed on top of your head.

The first two down downs usually go to the hares. Today it was Baldrick and his partner Slack Bladder. The Religious Adviser (RA)* Mr Magoo, a short Geordie with a generous figure, described the run, pointing out its salient features. 'It was a good run, short and hilly, but with far too many fish hooks and not enough short cuts. However the scenery was spectacular and we all feel the hares should be congratulated on their first laying of a trail'.

Snowman - average height, snow-coloured hair and a reasonably generous figure - was also given a down down for casting aspersions on the figure of the Religious Advisor. He had been discussing the previous weekend when one of the hash had seen the RA walking on Ryde beach. Snowman had the cheek to suggest that if the RA was seen too close to the shore Green Peace would drag him back into the water!

Steve Butler, a fast running slim whippet, was given a down down as he had just returned from Australia. Naturally he had to perform his down down while turned upside down.

There was also a virgin present (first time on a run!) but she was asked to watch the others to see how it was done.

The hash then sings a song;

The Religious Advisor presides over all hash formalities, introducing the hares at the start and telling amusing stories found in the press the week before. The RA told us about a trade dispute between France and America when George Bush is alleged to have remarked 'The trouble with the French is they have no word for Entrepreneur'

1: This is Hashing on the Isle of Wight

'They are hashers, they are blue
They are hashers through and through
They are arseholes so they say
And they'll never get to heaven in a long long way'

At this point those with down downs start drinking. Hard On, Dangerous and Lost Boy ably assist Steve Butler into an inverted position.

'Get it down down down down down' etc

Lots of rapid drinking takes place, although in Steve Butler's case most of it reappeared out of his nose or was spilt. Slack Bladder actually managed to beat Black Adder in drinking her pint of beer, so there were loud comments of 'Beaten by a woman!' (to the tune of nare nare na nare na) and other politically incorrect statements such as 'You great wuss!'

The next group of sinners was introduced. Flossing (Gorgeous blonde female who wore a thong on her first hash run, hence the name flossing!) received a down down for doing a short cut. Mongrel (whose name derives from her mixed ancestry, not to the incident of her dog trying to fly off Culver cliff),* for passing a NO DOGS ALLOWED notice. Navigator, for not going back on a fishhook, BT (short for big tits) got a down down of water because she avoided the ford.

I failed to drink all of the beer in my down down so poured the remainder over my head. From outside came the roar of motorbike engines and about twenty five rockers drew up in the car park.

This is a very sad story. BT volunteered to look after Mongrel's dog while she was away on holiday. It was a lovely golden retriever that used to run everywhere, full of life. BT took the dog for a walk up Culver Cliff above Sandown Bay. The dog was having fun chasing the rabbits that live in profusion on the grassy meadow at the top of the hill. The rabbits are very devious and use the cliff as a method of avoiding predators; they dig their burrows just under the lip of the vertical drop at the cliff edge. When the rabbits run into their burrows they look as though they are going over the cliff. Sadly the dog chased them and followed a perfect parabola as it fell to its death on the rocks below. BT phoned the Cliff Rescue to collect the dog's body and stored it in her freezer until Mongrel returned - she didn't want to spoil her holiday by telling her what had happened till she got back. (It gave Poor Sod one hell of a shock when he unwittingly opened the freezer to get something out for dinner!)

Several people looked around with a certain amount of apprehension. As this was a Bank Holiday weekend the rockers could be followed by a group of mods and all hell could break loose.

The rockers looked superb. dressed in serious leathers, clambering off their Harleys and BMWs all of which were immaculate; visions in shining paintwork and glistening chrome. As they walked in through the door it was clear that there wasn't going to be any trouble today. All of them were in their late fifties or early 60s, removing the Zimmer frame attachments from the back of their Harleys and ordering some Sanatogen tonic wine.'There would only be a rumble if a group of Mods came in with walking sticks and started spraying Deep Heat around!

We drove back to Ryde on the Newport Road passing the Eight Bells pub - famous for the quantity of its food portions and the river running at the end of its garden. Many a happy hour has been spent there watching the swans and ducks while enjoying an enormous ploughman's lunch. There is something really magical about sitting in a pub with a river running past. Pubs, I feel, are great places anyway but to be able to enjoy glorious scenery and have the sound of a river babbling past is something special.

The road leads on to Newport, the capital of the Isle of Wight. It is still possible to see the Victorian terrace houses along the High Street if you look above the glass shop fronts. There are no shopping malls here - the shopping centre is a throwback to the 1950s.

There is a pedestrianised area around St Thomas's church where there are shops selling jewellery, paintings and leather goods. Opposite the church is Gods Providence meeting house. This has been converted to a restaurant where they do some wonderful homemade food. I can highly recommend the vegetable soup and the Quiche. This is not mass produced standard food but individually cooked and delicious. It is a great shame that so many restaurants are going over to heating up food that is cooked in a factory and delivered to their door. Wherever you go in the country, you get the same fare, no cooking skills or individuality required.

At the bottom of the High street is the main traffic island, known as Rubics roundabout to locals. It is a huge three lane beast with traffic lights set up every 50 yards; it is almost impossible to get in the right lane and often, when aiming to go to Cowes, you find yourself

1: This is Hashing on the Isle of Wight

heading for Sandown or turning into the multiplex cinema and watching a film!

The road to Ryde leads past Medina arboretum ('I walked around the place for hours and couldn't find the arboretum anywhere - it was just a load of trees' Snowman's quote of the week!)

On the way back to Ryde we passed over Wooton Creek: the road is built on a low bridge with a lake on one side and a small river estuary on the left. There are many yachts moored here as there is easy access to the Solent. Driving over the creek we met Isle of Wight Piltdown man. He has a skinhead hair cut; is built like a gorilla and drives a white van which he parks in the middle of the road blocking as much traffic as possible.

A polite request to move was greeted with the traditional two-finger salute and he continued his conversation with a female vision of tattoos and hundreds of body piercings who would only be attractive to a magnet! However Isle of Wight Piltdown man is afraid of fire and flashing blue lights. It was very satisfying when a police car drew up behind us and told him in no uncertain terms that he was causing an obstruction. Who says you can never find a policeman when you want one!

Chapter 2

Corfe Farm Run

I picked up Fracas from his house in Ryde to take him across to West Wight and a run set by Shergar. I should have had more sense really and stayed in bed (he isn't called Shergar because he runs slowly!) The sun was shining brightly from a deep blue sky with an occasional fluffy cloud on the horizon. It was a weak, cold sun that shone down on us. The depth of atmosphere it was shining through on this spring day had dissipated all of its energy.

Even so, it was still a glorious morning and we decided to take the scenic route across to the West Wight. We headed out of Ryde along the Ashey road and over the downs. I tried to get some fuel on the way but the garage was closed. The warning light had been on for a while and we were driving on vapour! We made a detour through Newchurch where I knew there was a garage. However, my knowledge of the local area was not as good as I thought. The garage had become a block of flats - I must have driven through there six times in the last year and never noticed!

The fuel situation was getting serious; we did not want to break down in the West Wight - they barbeque unaccompanied strangers over there! Fracas decided we should go through Godshill where there was bound to be a garage open. Godshill is a very pretty thatched tourist trap. It is actually quite tastefully done for a tourist village -

the thatched cottages are well looked after and not too twee. There is a Cider barn selling locally produced cider, with lots of arty shops selling paintings and jewellery; it is thankfully free of the T-shirt tat that is often found in similar mainland locations.

The church stands majestically on the hill. However the Vicarage has in its garden the smallest model village I have ever seen. How they have the cheek to charge people to see it I do not know. We found a garage that was clearly part of a farm; some entrepreneurial farmer had converted one of his fields to a forecourt and garage. We were very relieved to fill up with diesel even though grazing heifers surrounded us.

Heading into Godshill we got as far as the Griffin pub then turned left down Beacon Alley. This is a glorious one-track road with the trees almost meeting overhead. It all forms the sort of wooded tunnel that Frodo galloped down while escaping black riders in the Lord of the Rings. The sun played dancing shadows on the trees - it was very pretty.

We arrived at Corfe Farm just down the road from Chale Green. Shergar led us up a vertical incline into a very muddy field. The Rover complained as the exhaust scraped along the ground. We parked at the top and the view was spectacular; the white cliffs of Freshwater Bay glinting in the distance; rolling fields in all directions.

The On On was downhill through serious shiggy (thick mud) and across the farmyard. The trail then headed down towards a lake and we went three quarters of the way around it. Then we had to cross a muddy stream. It was just about possible to cross it by jumping if you had a good run up. Otherwise you ended up in about 50 cm (1.5 feet) of mud. Fracas was in a playful mood and was looking for Hooker to throw into the water. Hooker could not be found so he settled for giving Boycey a gentle push as she made her run up. She ended up soaked to the knees and told Fracas he was very naughty, or some words to that effect, but ending in 'ard'! After my jump I managed to cut my hand open so deeply that it would not stop bleeding. I spent the next mile worrying about tetanus.

We ran on through sparsely wooded tracks just talking to anyone who happened to be running at the same speed and laughing at all those keen runners who had to come back on a fish hook. I was at the back chatting to Sunker (she is small dark haired and very fit; she

2: Corfe Farm Run

must have had an off-day as she was at the back), about how if the Isle of Wight were placed on its edge in the sea it would be possible to climb up it and arrive in space. Space is only twenty five miles upwards - what a frightening thought! As the fish hookers appeared we ran slowly along, making sure that they all had to go past us right to the back.*

However, it did not take long for the fishhook runners to end up back at the front. They turned round ran past us up a steep incline and were at the front of the pack again faster than you can say Hash House Harrier. Boycey even managed to get caught on a fishhook twice.

Boycey really is an excellent example of what hashing can do for fitness levels. She only started running with us about two years ago and she used to walk along very slowly at the back. She could not even keep up with me, so she must have been unfit. She kept coming each week and now she runs nearly all the way at the front of the pack.

We came to another stream with a bridge across it. The bridge was lined out and standing in the middle of the water was Tannoy, announcing to P-rick† that he was a wimp not to jump across. In fact her Golden Retriever (Bell) was jumping backwards and forwards across the gap showing P-rick exactly what to do. Whenever P-rick got anywhere near the water Tannoy would send sheets of water into the air in his direction. He just went for it in the end. He stood in the middle of the stream with Tannoy and they soaked each other completely. We ran on along the flat for another two miles then started to climb up a gentle incline.

We got to the top of a hill and admired the view of farmland rolling into the distance, and the sea sparkling. The sun was still shining where we were but a big black cloud was rushing towards us at high speed. We could all see the cars about 2 miles away on the opposite side of the valley. 'What happens if it rains?' asked one of the newer hash members. 'We get wet', I told her rather heartlessly.

---

* *On a fish hook the first five runners have to go to the back of the pack ie the last person who is still running. Walkers do not count.*

† *P-rick; his name is probably one of the few that have been given in a hash even before the person has done one run. On his first ever run he registered with Fracas who asked his name. Being Ex military P-rick said 'Pearson Richard' and almost added Sir! Fracas didn't hear so asked him again 'Pearson Rick' he said. 'Ah P. Rick' said Fracas and it has stuck ever since!*

The cloud overtook us after about 10 minutes and all hell broke loose. It went dark and started to rain as though it was the monsoon season in the tropics. It rapidly changed into hail that was blown into our faces by the wind and suddenly it was absolutely freezing. The only thing to do was to keep running; it was either that or die of exposure. The last mile back to the cars was hell on legs I arrived shivering and staggering from exhaustion! But in a funny way I was elated, there is nothing like a battle with the elements to give you an adrenalin rush!

We got changed out of muddy running gear and I drove to the Three Bishops pub in Brighstone - my kind of pub, with oak beams; a roaring log fire; large enough to cater for diners in the front bar and traditional drinkers like the hash in the back. It is a very welcoming place with friendly bar staff and efficient waitresses.

The down downs were presided over by P-rick. Rainmaker (another very pretty blonde female) was given one for dancing a jig (doing a rain dance) just before the hail came down. Baldrick was given one for getting lost and turning up to the pub late. I was given a watery one for being a "virgin" (well, I had not been on a run for so long no one recognised me).

Mr Unappreciative was given one for being surprisingly unappreciative. He, P-rick and a few others had gone on the Leap Year Day hash. Rainmaker had offered to give them a lift from the end of the pier on their return. They got back late and when they rang her up she had to get out of bed to collect them. When she saw their T shirts she really liked the Lord of the Rings style design. She asked Mr Unappreciative if she could have one. 'Yes,' he said in a very drunken state 'You can either pay £7.50 or give me a blow job!' She declined to do either

Hooker was then given one for asking when was the Leap Year Day hash!

Returning to Ryde a pleasant afternoon was enjoyed by all the Ryde hashers at Salvatori's Restaurant. This is a superb Italian restaurant, run efficiently by the proprietor Salvatori, the husband of Boycey, and his cooking is terrific. The restaurant is situated on St Johns Hill, Ryde and is a beautifully proportioned building shaped a little like a swan's nest.

2: Corfe Farm Run

I can recommend without hesitation all of his food, but the antipasta starter is something special and his steak in cream and brandy sauce is an experience of gastronomic levels.

We met Fraca's wife (Di) their son (Tom) and his girlfriend Nicki. Tom and Nicki had just returned from a holiday in the Far East. They visited the site of the Selangor Club, Kuala Lumpur and saw the area where the hash was first set up by Gisbert.* They then travelled on to Japan were Nicki had experienced the gourmet delights of sperm from a whale. Not usual in Europe as a starter, it is apparently very common in Japan. She remarked, 'I go away on holiday for a few weeks with my boyfriend and come back absolutely stuffed full of sperm!' There is not a lot you can say to that!

Tom and Nicki were told all about the history of hashing while they were in Kuala Lumpur. How in 1938 a group of ex-patriots started a running club. It was very similar to the paper chases popular in Public schools of the day. (See Tom Brown's School Days.)

The idea was for a hare to set a trail laid in paper or flour and for the others to follow the trail attempting to catch the hare. The concept was adapted by A.S Gisbert who made the chase non-competitive. They ran around the local area in order to 'earn their lunch' at the Selangor Club, known as the Hash House because of its appalling food.

The name Hash House Harriers was introduced to the world in 1938, and from then it has gone from strength to strength.

Today it is reckoned that there are at least 1500 hashes and a total of 200 000 hashers world-wide.

Chapter 3

Yorkshire - Queen's Golden Jubilee Hash

Yorkshire - God's own county is a bloody long way from the Isle of Wight, so my wife, Hyacinth (She is just like Mrs Bucket from Keeping Up Appearances as far as hashing is concerned), and I decided to do it in two sections. We drove up on the Friday night to Sutton Coldfield, Birmingham.

We all went for a meal at the Shimla restaurant in Mere Green - as far as I am concerned it is one of the best curry houses in Birmingham. You can taste a hint of vinegar in the vindaloo, giving it a hot but authentic flavour. They do a fantastic stuffed pepper starter filled with spicy vegetables or mincemeat. The quality of the meat is superb; it just melts in your mouth.

I am probably one of the few people in the world that love Birmingham. The people are friendly (well, those you can understand!) There is a huge diversity in the population and this produces a very multicultural city.

It has had a massive revival since the days when it was a "dirty old town" an industrial sprawl with the Bull Ring as its main attraction.

I must admit that when I was growing up there in the '70s' the city centre was an ugly place. Given over totally to the motorcar, pedestrians were forced down rat hole underpasses and the smell of exhaust fumes was everywhere.

I remember going on a student canal boat trip from Gas Street Basin. The water of the canal was black and turgid and there were old supermarket trolleys and used condoms dumped in the cut. The whole area was made up of warehouses that blotted out the sky and towered over the side of the canal. This was only ten minutes walk from the city centre! The place, for all its industrial heritage, had no soul. No one seemed proud of it.

Now it has gone through a huge revival. Thanks to some superb decisions made by the local authority during the 80s and 90s, Birmingham just buzzes. Gas Street Basin has now been converted into a boat haven with wonderful pubs and cafes along the side, where one can sit out and watch the water. Flats along the edge of the canal now go for £300 000: people actually go fishing in the water and don't just catch black ribbed knoblers!

The Malt house pub that Bill Clinton went into with Tony Blair during a G7 meeting now stands proudly on the edge of the canal. I was told a story where it was alleged that when Bill Clinton had finished with his drink the security men took his glass away and completely destroyed it (much to the chagrin of the bar maid). They told the barmaid that as it had the president's fingerprints on it had to be completely obliterated. I told this story to a fellow hasher who commented 'I hope they didn't have to do the same thing to Monica Lewinsky's breasts!'

There is the Sea Life Centre (as far away from the sea as you can get in England! Amazing!) The National Convention Centre, the Symphony Hall, are all built in the area that used to be so desolate. Just across the road is the Repertory theatre: Centenary Square, just outside the Rep, has wonderful sculptures and waterfalls; paved and grass areas with plenty of seating where you can just watch the world go by. Massive celebrations go on there every New Years Eve and outdoor concerts are a regular occurrence.

There are Chinese restaurants, curry houses, Mexican, Indonesian cafes, clubs bars even a Ronnie Scott's jazz club - all within stag-

3: Yorkshire - Queen's Golden Jubilee Hash

gering distance. This is not even the city centre. However, it is possible to walk from The Repertory theatre into and across the entire city centre without once crossing a road. Try doing that in central London! Gone are the days when pedestrians were made to walk down rat holes.

The walkway goes towards the Copthorne Hotel and into an enclosed glass area that is actually the inner courtyard of the main city library. There are bars and shops; a Mc Donald's, a Pizzeria and various other fast food outlets. The library is a bit of an eyesore - 70s concrete never seems to work. However, as a building, it is pretty unique. It has reversed tiers of glass and concrete, forming a rectangle around a central courtyard. This is supposed to allow large amounts of natural light to get into the reading areas from both sides of the building. Doesn't seem to work for me: I would have thought a normal pyramid would let in far more light. But what do I know?

However as you come out onto Victoria Square you notice that this 70s obelisk is surrounded by beautiful Victorian buildings. It really looks incredibly incongruous. The town hall; the natural history museum; the old concert hall; all surround a tiered square with an enormous waterfall at its centre. There is a statue of a naked woman in the pool at the top - described locally as the floozy in the Jacuzzi.

I can highly recommend Birmingham's Natural History Museum. It is one of the most wonderful places to take the kids on a wet Saturday afternoon. There are stuffed animals, dinosaurs that move and make noises, minerals that glow under ultraviolet light, insects, reptiles and ancient pottery. What's more, admission is free! Sadly, since I have been writing, the Natural History Museum has gone. All the exhibits moved to the Millennium Point where, of course, you have to pay lots of money to get in.

A large rusty iron figure stands at the bottom of the square showing the way to the new Bull Ring. Walking along a now pedestrianised Corporation Street, there are more shops than you can shake a stick at. There is a very impressive Dillon's bookshop in an old Midland Bank building. The architecture inside is amazing with a glass cupola at the top. If you fancy a quiet drink, there is the Bacchus Theme Bar, part of the Burlington Hotel, all done in different themed alcoves: Greek, Egyptian, English Aristocratic, Cluedo Type Library, and Medieval.

Just across the road is The Wellington pub famous for its vast array of real ales. There are so many of them that they are listed on TV monitors and you just ask for the beer you want by number.

As you continue down past the Odeon Cinema and into the new Bull Ring,* the size of the place is staggering, with three massive floors of solid retail therapy.

The Selfridges building is instantly recognisable from the outside (it looks like an alien space ship that has just landed), being blue, and covered in aluminium circles; inside it is an open plan department store. The bottom floor has every conceivable type of food for sale. There is a sushi bar, just like the one Johnny English made famous by getting his tie stuck in the moving conveyor belt.

There is a coffee bar that has technology that would not look out of place on the Starship Enterprise – boilers, chrome pipes, digital displays and filters that make coffee that is just........., well, try it!

You can see up through the rest of the building from every floor, as the sales area is only around the outside of a huge open space. It must have been a brave decision to make about thirty percent of the building into open space that cannot be used to display merchandise. However I feel it is wonderful; there is none of the stuffy confined feelings you get in the old style department stores.

Birmingham's incredible construction, the

The next day Hyacinth and I set out up the M6. This is very frustrating; even on a Saturday morning it is packed with vehicles, and progress out of Birmingham towards Stafford is made at a snails pace. We eventually arrived at the M62 turned off and headed for Yorkshire. About half way along this stretch of road there is a farmhouse on the central reservation of the motorway - a very strange place to live. I do not know why it was not compulsorily purchased but it has sound-proofing on the windows and the farmer has a tunnel for his sheep.

The road then becomes surrounded by stunning scenery which goes right across the top of the Pennines. The views on either side are

---

When it was under construction, the Bullring was the largest building project in Europe. It cost 500 Million to construct. It has lots of open spaces, walkways and event areas, unlike most other shopping centres. It covers an area of over 110 000 square metres and contains over 100 shops. No I am not being paid any money by the BullRing Corporation I just think it is a great place, a wonderful improvement on the dilapidated old 1960s Bullring Centre.

3: Yorkshire - Queen's Golden Jubilee Hash

spectacular - mountains going into the distance with deep valleys in between. At the bottom of the valleys are lakes and reservoirs sparkling in the sun.

It was a glorious summer's day and we could see for miles. We passed under the elegant footbridge that carries the Pennine Way across the motorway and the hikers waved back to us as we wind milled at them through the window.

We came across the M606 and turned off to Bradford all of a sudden, probably because we were not paying attention, and drove down the familiar roads where we had both been students for many years. The smell of curry pervaded the air and we were tempted to stop, but decided we must not be too late for the hash registration. Bradford had not really changed in the 20 years since we had lived there. It was still very run down We passed oases of development - the Museum of the Moving Image, the elegant Alhambra theatre, and headed across town on the road towards Saltaire (named after Sir Titus Salt) and Howarth.

Sir Titus Salt was a model mill owner who really treated his employees well, providing good accommodation, free health care and education - all in the village that he built around his mill. However, working for him came at a cost; he was a devout Christian and did not allow anyone to drink or have fun of any kind. It seems strange today to think that your employer could actually run your life, tell you what you are allowed to drink and where you should go during your leisure time.*

On arriving at Howarth I changed into low gear as we went down the incredibly steep road leading to the centre of town. We continued through the valley and up the other side past the Bronte parsonage. The moor looked anything but cold and bleak basking in the sunshine. I pictured Heathcliffe sunbathing on the springy grass rather than coming out of a forbidding mist on a cold night.

---

* Then again perhaps it is not so odd. Even today contracts of employment usually have clauses stating that you are not allowed to take any paid work during your leisure time without your employer's permission. Modern day contracts do not state working hours and people can be asked to come in at weekends or during holidays or at an employer's whim. Even the working hours directive can be opted out of and I know many people who have had to opt out if they wanted any chance of promotion in their line of work. This is simply not fair and it is about time the government did something about it!

Howarth is really quaint - stone houses and cottages with a steam railway running along the valley floor. There are lots of superb pubs to choose from, the Black Bull pub, with its ghostly manifestations, being the best in my view. It is a wonderful traditional pub, all polished woods and comfortable chairs. It also has several ghosts. In fact I felt something touch me on the head as I walked into the place it felt really strange.

Hyacinth thought I was mad However one of the guys by the bar said. 'Oh that will be old Bramwell Bronte, he was the brother of the Bronte sisters. He often touches people as they walk in, usually if he likes them. Bramwell was one of those funny handshake blokes, they used to have lodge meetings here in the 1800s, you're not a mason are you?'

Apparently Bramwell drank himself senseless in the pub and died in 1849. He is buried in Howarth church. The chair at the top of the stairs is supposedly infused with his spirit.

Other ghosts have been seen sitting at a table in the bar one is thought to be Dan Sugden who was the landlord when Bramwell used to frequent the pub. There are also reported sightings of several ghosts that walk through walls.

We were told that the light above the Bronte picture often moves by itself at night. All this haunting is caused by the graveyard at the back of the pub, which is built on a slope. Many of the bodies are thought to have slid down under the foundations of the pub.

We booked into our B and B; dumped our gear and drove the mile or so out onto the moor where the hash was based. This was a youth hostel with plenty of camping space overlooking the Watersheddles Reservoir. It was deserted; all the hash must be running or at the pub we surmised. We drove down the road and the first pub we came to contained a hundred singing hashers. We got some drinks and sat in the garden - it was very pleasant if a little vocally challenged!

Twonk, the hash Neolithic man was there looking a little worse for wear. Mongrel was recounting some story about how she got lost on the hash, misplaced her running shoe then got a lift back on a tractor. Five Bar and Miss Whiplash told us what a good run it had been, very steep and long but excellent scenery.

3: Yorkshire - Queen's Golden Jubilee Hash

The climb back up to the youth hostel from where we were was almost vertical and all of them wanted a lift. We just about managed to get them in by sitting on each other's knees.

On our return we bumped into P-rick who said he had been asked to do a bit of painting and decorating this evening by a group of the girls. He said he didn't like DIY but they told him to come along, as he would definitely enjoy it. Intrigued he had agreed to help out.

We had a few beers and discussed our tactics for the evening with Pat (Tanglefoot) and Chris (Godot). We were all republicans and did not want to celebrate the Queen's Golden Jubilee. The evening party looked as though it was all going to be Union Jacks and 'God bless the Queen' memorabilia. I had made some large badges with a picture of a guillotine and the statement '**BE A CITIZEN NOT A SUBJECT.**' We all wore these with pride although it was possible we would be lynched by some of the more monarchy minded hashers.

The dance area was done out as predicted – flags, pictures of the Queen and lots of golden jubilee tat everywhere. There was a huge picture of Her Majesty on the back wall completely dominating the dance floor.

It was a gorgeous summer's evening and we wandered around the site chatting to friends and winding up monarchists. The views across the moors were stunning as the sun set in a blaze of glory, reflecting red light on the waters of the reservoir. I thought 'Well, there are worse places to be on a Saturday night.' The atmosphere was intoxicating. There was a buzz from everyone; they were out to have a good time and relax. This is what hashing is all about!

P-rick reappeared, looking a little nervous. He announced that before the disco started there was going to be a cabaret presented by some of the girls. We were all intrigued so we went up to the dance floor to see what was happening. The Girls all appeared wearing dresses made out of Union Jack flags with Union Jack hats. They didn't seem to be wearing much else.

They did a terrific dance routine to the tune of *I want you to ride my bicycle* by Queen. As the music faded away they took off the top half of their dresses to reveal some interesting breasts. They all had perfect Union Jacks painted on their breasts and nipples all different sizes and moving in unison to the music. This received some tumultuous applause and many calls of encore.

The music then started in earnest and I wandered over to chat to P-rick. 'Interesting show the girls put on!' I said. 'By the way, how did you get on with the painting and decorating?' I asked. 'Who do you think helped to paint some of the Union Jacks on the breasts?' he said

You're joking!' I said. 'No!' he said. 'It took me nearly two hours to complete but it must have been one of the best two hours of my life, I have still got an erection the size of the Thames barrage. You would not believe how difficult it is to paint neatly over wobbly bits. The times I had to wipe it all off and start again! It was tough!' he said. Perhaps he doth complain too much I thought. The only words I could say really were 'You lucky bastard!'

We went for a bop around on the dance floor and a Yorkshire hasher called Magnum appeared. Yes, he is the spitting image of Tom Sellick; he even works for the police force. I don't know quite how to describe what he was wearing. I want you to imagine Magnum PI wearing a gold body suit with gold leggings. Stuffed down the front of these were 3 pairs of socks giving him bulges in all the wrong places. On his feet were gold boots with golden tassels. A gold medallion and a fur stole completed the outfit that was topped off with a gold wig; he really looked like Midas on a bad day. However he thought it was worth showing off and he danced the night away - a vision in gold.

The next morning the Sunday run was from the camp site. We set off down the hill and across on to the moor; it was hot and several hashers fell by the wayside suffering from heat stroke and dehydration. They retired to the pub to get some liquid inside them!

I continued along, climbing up a steep rock face and passing a lake or two. We eventually came out at the Bronte Falls. These are a series of little waterfalls cascading down the hill and ending in small pools. It was an idyllic scene; there were lots of children playing in the water. The sun was shining and the views were glorious.

The On In was arduous as we had all the downhill bit on the way out. It was a solid slog up very steep hills back to the campsite. I arrived exhausted so we had a rest before going to the Bronte Parsonage

3: Yorkshire - Queen's Golden Jubilee Hash

Museum. This is a wonderful place to visit. It is preserved as it would have looked in the 1800s. There are twelve rooms to look around and it gives a real flavour of what life was like for the Bronte sisters growing up with their kindly father The Revd. Patrick Brontë.

The evening we spent on a pub-crawl around Howarth. It has a vast array of pleasant hostelries and I enjoyed it so much that I can actually remember very little about it!

We set out on Monday morning looking forward to a Bradford curry. I do not know what they put in the curries from Bradford but they are definitely addictive. We get cravings for them that have to be satisfied on a regular basis. We headed straight for Great Horton road, home of the University of Bradford and of the Shimla curry house.

The Shimla seems to be the only spit and sawdust curry house left - the rest have gone up market. I noticed that they still did the UBAC curry. This was devised by the University of Bradford Alcoholics and Curry Society. To become a member you had to eat two UBACS and drink ten pints of beer in one night - not easy as the UBAC is astonishingly hot and very filling.

The Shimla does not provide knives and forks; the food is eaten straight from the bowl using Chapattis. A starter of onions and a slice of tomato in a mint yogurt sauce are given as a side dish. This is however liberally sprinkled with chilli so even the cooling yoghurt tends to blow your head off. You rapidly empty the complimentary jug of water.

The taste of the curry is fantastic I had the Keema (unnamed variety of mince)* madras these mince dishes are really spicy but taste almost of toffee and just slide down. Hyacinth had Chicken madras in a really thick sauce which was gorgeous.

The temperature of the curries is unbelievable; a Madras in Bradford is like a Phall anywhere else. Many an innocent traveller has been caught out. Those used to a Vindaloo from their local take away in the south have been left unable to breathe and end up with numb faces after ordering a vindaloo from a Bradford curry house. The cost of this very filling meal was three pounds each, excellent value.

---

* *One of the curry houses in Bradford was closed down for serving Kangaroo meat. Where they got it from no one knows!*

Next door is The Shearbridge pub a typical student haunt. We hoped to bring back those memories of student life. I remember many happy hours drinking in the Shearbridge; groups of students putting the world to rights. It was always packed and there was always a group of old Yorkshire men playing dominoes at the table in the corner. They were completely oblivious to the student mayhem around them.

However, now we could not believe the age of the students; they looked about ten years old, only just out of short trousers. In these familiar surrounding we remembered being students but realised that twenty years takes its toll. You can't turn back the clock! I suppose that by now the domino players have all died; it is very sad.

Chapter 4

Holmfirth

We drove out of Bradford in melancholy mood and headed for Holmfirth, the Yorkshire town where *Last of the Summer Wine* is filmed. It is a typical dales town with stone built terrace houses running down steep hills, set in typical Yorkshire countryside. Alongside the main street flows a small river that has featured in many an episode.

I remember one episode where Compo is testing out a submarine made out of an old tin bath. Somehow the magic of television produced a scene where the submarine goes under the water and only the periscope is visible, spying on Howard and Marina. How this is achieved I have no idea, as the water is only about two feet deep along the entire length of the river.

Sid's café is real, and outside there is a model of Compo; and many of the cast are featured in photographs. Inside the café is absolutely tiny and the counter is in the wrong place. They must use wide-angle lenses and mix shots in from the studio.

Nora Batty's house is also real but is a private dwelling and the owners seem to be a bit fed up with all the tourists peering in through the windows. Where Compo lives in the series is actually a *Last of the Summer Wine Museum* with lots of photographs and memorabilia of the series.

There are buses that take you on a guided tour of all the locations used for filming. Clegg's house is actually miles outside the town as is Wesley's garage. The pubs they go into are all there and the countryside feels familiar because of watching the series. Thirty years of the television series must have done wonders for Holmfirth's tourist trade.

On the way back through Birmingham we went to visit my father's plaque in Sutton Coldfield Crematorium. It has a photo of him on it and the words.

Roy Williams born on the 9th of June 1922

Died on his son's 43rd Birthday, 11th of November 2001

A great character who loved life, golf and beer.

Sadly missed by his family and friends.

He was an amazing character who became a little eccentric, as he got older. I remember when his second wife Doreen died he really was in a state, so I drove up to Southport to help him to sort everything out. Doreen had really done everything domestic for him. He had no idea how to use the cooker. The washing machine was a complete mystery and, worst of all, he had let the cat escape. This was a beautiful female Siamese that was Doreen's pride and joy.

We sorted out all the funeral arrangements together. I then went through the operation of the cooker and we did some experimental loads of washing. By the third load Dad was getting bored and decided it was time to go for a beer. I jogged along behind dad's electric buggy that really could motor - a top speed of 15 miles per hour.

He would call to pedestrians 'Out of my way! Coming through!' honking his horn. Old ladies with Zimmer frames would jump into the road, narrowly avoiding collisions with oncoming lorries. We went down the road to the Mount Pleasant pub, which is one of the few places left in Southport where you can have a beer and a quiet conversation.

We ordered some food and a pint or two. Dad seemed to be getting more relaxed so I got some more beers in. This was 5.30 pm; by about 10 pm we had drank far too much. Dad was telling me how he had not really got on with Doreen over the last few years and he was

4: Holmfirth

certain that she would come back and haunt him. He kept talking about 'true' ghost stories he had seen on television. I tried to convince him that ghosts did not exist but he was having none of it.

We headed back to his house, he driving erratically and taking out the occasional slow moving pedestrian, me staggering along behind. On arriving home dad decided to go straight to bed and was asleep almost immediately. I could hear snoring coming through the wall. I looked around the room where I was sleeping and realised that it was Doreen's old room and that the bedding had not been changed since she died. I could clearly see some of her hairs on the pillow.

I should have thought about this earlier when I realised Dad could not use the washing machine. No problem I thought through an alcoholic haze I will just find some clean sheets and change the bed. Well I searched everywhere and could find nothing. I was still feeling very drunk so I just gave up, lay on the floor and tried to get to sleep. This was not easy as the floor was not comfortable and the room felt occupied by someone other than me! Eventually I drifted off and dreamt of ghostly apparitions chasing me round the house.

I awoke in the middle of the night to a really weird sound. I heard Dad through the wall saying, 'Oh, you're back! Ohhhh! Ohhhhhh! It's great, you're back!' I could feel the hairs on the back of my neck standing up with superstitious dread. My whole body was in a cold sweat. I even pinched myself to make sure I wasn't still dreaming. The lamp by the bed would not work and it was pitch black. 'Oh, it's so lovely to see you' came through the wall. I staggered out of bed and scrambled for the light switch. It took an eternity to find it but eventually I could see and opened the door. 'I have missed you so much!' came from Dad's room as I walked into the hall.

'Dad!' I said. 'w..who are you talking to?' I nervously opened the door and walked into Dad's bedroom. Look, Mark!' he said. 'She's back!' I looked down on the bed and saw the cat had returned!

Chapter 5

Carisbrook Castle Run

Summer was in the air when a small pack of about 25 hashers parked at the Nunnery car park, Carisbrook Castle. It felt like June with a hot sun blazing down on the assembled throng. The castle is wonderfully preserved, brooding majestically over the surrounding countryside.

Carisbrook is a medieval castle that was built on the site of an old Roman fortification. Charles the first was held prisoner there before he was taken to London to have his height reduced. An attempt to escape was foiled when he got stuck in the bars.

The castle has also been used as the residence of the governor of the Isle of Wight and was home to princess Beatrice, youngest daughter of Queen Victoria.

The only problem with starting a run from a castle is that the start of the run is all downhill which inevitably means the end of the run will be all uphill. The run was set by Gisbert the hash haberdash named because he looks like the original hash founder in Malaysia (A S Gisbert). However, there have been recent attempts to change his name to Pike as he often acts like the *Dads Army* character. On the Vectis Lunatics run (they only run on a night when there is a full moon) he got up out of his seat in the pub and rushed straight into the ladies' loo. This was only two seconds after Flossing had made the same mistake with the Gents (they were close together and not well labelled). The cry of 'You stupid boy!' rang throughout the pub. I feel a renaming coming on.

We ran down the hill going West of Carisbrook and then turned right along a public footpath heading towards Newport. As we travelled along the top ridge we saw below us a grand Victorian building that was in exactly the same style as Birmingham University (I wonder if it was the same Victorian architect).

I had not passed this way before and asked Gisbert what it was. 'It's Whitecroft, the loony bin,' he stated in one of his less politically correct statements. 'It is amazingly large, considering the population of the Isle of Wight is only about 250 00 people,' I said. 'Yes, it is,' said a passing hasher 'the Isle of Wight is beautiful but it has one of the largest mental health problems per head of population in the country no one seems to know why?'

We passed to the bottom of the valley and there was the sound of dogs barking and howling from a large house set back from the road. 'Is that a kennels?' asked Fracas. 'No, it's the home of the local hunt,' said Alan. They keep the hounds in there and then take them out on a Saturday to murder a few foxes.'

'I can't stand them!' said Floss. 'It's is horrible.' They seem to have no control over the hounds or the horses. I was almost run down by one of them coming around a corner last week.' 'Yep it's the sort of idiots that go hunting, they're usually so busy trying to grow chins that they can't keep their eyes on the path in front of them!' said a passing hasher who will remain nameless.

After this the talking stopped as the hill in front of us stretched for miles up to the castle. It is easy to tell when you are actually improving your fitness level on a run - it is when the talking stops.

We went to some awful pub on Newport Town High Street for the après. Not my type of place. It had large screens showing sports matches, plastic tables and chairs, no garden, and nowhere you can have a quiet conversation. I couldn't really hear the down downs as they were blotted out by the noise of some football match.

Chapter 6

Cherbourg

The annual IOW hash trip to France usually takes place in September. It is organised superbly by Steve and Carol Taverner (Loading Bay and Poubelle). This year we were going to Cherbourg. The plan was to catch the *Pride of Bilbao* from Portsmouth on Friday night (known locally as the party boat), sail overnight with a cabin on board, and arrive refreshed the next day.

We caught the Wightlink catamaran service from Ryde pier head to Portsmouth harbour and then had a mini bus provided to take us to the International ferry port about 3 miles away. There was not enough room on the mini bus so Carol (Poubell) being very fit decided to jog. The traffic through Portsmouth on a Friday night was such that the mini bus and Carol both arrived at the Port simultaneously.

We waited in the bar with crowds of other partygoers all dressed for the 70s theme night. There were Hen night and Stag night groups; people celebrating birthdays - some were dressed as Vikings for some bizarre reason - all waiting in the very overcrowded bar for a beer, or the opening of the doors for embarkation.

The *Pride of Bilboa* is enormous, probably the largest Ferry operating in the English Channel. It has at least 6 bars, 5 restaurants; a pizza place for snacks; swimming pool; sauna and a choice of 4 cinemas. However, the actual cabins are tiny. I was sharing a case with my wife, so it was huge; there was not room for the case and the two of us standing up at the same time. I do not know why women need to bring the kitchen sink along when going away for a weekend. Perhaps it is because they are chained to it! It was fun to explore and most of the hash settled in the quiet bar after a quick exploration.

As the ferry set off with several whoops from the horn I went on the top deck and watched Portsmouth slip by. The Naval dockyard is always interesting: several destroyers were at anchor and the aircraft carrier Ark Royal was berthed up beside the last Quay. We could just see the masts of Nelsons Victory peaking over the top of the buildings: legend has it that Nelson's body was preserved in Brandy as the ship returned after his last fateful voyage.

Next came HMS Warrior the world's first Ironclad warship We slipped slowly past the new Gunwharf Keys development built on an old Naval dockyard: a large shopping complex with designer clothes for sale at bargain prices. On to old Portsmouth with its high defensive walls. The Still and West pub situated at the end of the wall is right next to the main shipping channel. It is an incredible experience to be sitting at a window seat as a large ship comes past. They just blot out the sky and the whole pub vibrates. Just past the shingle beach on the left is the old tunnel that Nelson used to go through to avoid crowds of onlookers when he was going out to sea.

In front of us is the first of the sea forts built at enormous cost during the Napoleonic wars; they never fired a shot in anger and became known as Palmerston's Follies. However, the walls are so thick that any modern missile would just bounce off. The second fort along, Spit Bank, has inside it a fresh water well. This astonishes me; the hole was dug through the base of the fort ie under the seawater, then continued down to a fresh water source under the Solent The third fort has been converted to a millionaire's mansion with a recording studio, swimming pool and helicopter pad. It is one of the few residences in the country where you do not have to pay rates.

I returned below decks and we went in search of food. We decided to go into the best restaurant on board and although we had to queue for a table the food was fairly good and we both enjoyed a bottle of St Emillion to wash it all down.

6: Cherbourg

The nightclub was in full swing when we got there and the hash were dancing away like demons. The dance floor was full to capacity and the movement of the ship made it difficult not to bump into others. One of the Vikings used this as an opportunity to keep bashing into the Pneumatic woman opposite. It wasn't subtle, but it worked and he disappeared with her back to his cabin later that night.

The atmosphere was great and I thought it would be a good idea to get a few more San Miguel beers in. The plan for an early night faded into the subconscious and when I next looked at my watch it was 2 am. 'What time do we need to be up tomorrow?' I asked one of the security staff.'5.30 am' he announced with glee. 'You are joking!' I said 'It's 2 am now, that's 3 and a half hours sleep.' 'That's right' he said clearly impressed with my mathematics. We went back to the cabin, squeezed around the huge case and climbed into bed.

DING DONG 'Good morning', announced the public address system 'Breakfast is now being served in the....' 'Bollocks! What is the time?' I asked to the world in general '5.30 said Hyacinth from the bunk below.' I ranted to the world about why I had not gone to bed earlier; why the ferries have to arrive at such a ridiculous hour in the morning, and how I would like to murder all those involved in the manufacture of San Miguel.

We headed out for breakfast, which was not the cheapest food I have eaten. Cooperman took out a second mortgage in order to purchase a full English breakfast. The ferry docked and we went out into the bright September sunshine, ouch, to look for a taxi. I knew that the hash did not look very well. However compared to some of those waiting in the taxi queue we were glowing with health. One of the Vikings from the stag night was lying on the floor with drooping horns, hoping that he would be taken to Valhalla soon.

The taxi took us into Cherbourg town centre where we were booked into the hotel Du Louvre on the Rue Henri Dunanat just down a small road from the statue of Napoleon on his horse. This was a super place and good value for money. There was no way we could go to our rooms at the unearthly hour of 8.30am. However, they had a room by the reception desk where we could leave our luggage and they served some wicked coffee that rejuvenated mind, body and soul. Fracas, Lady Di, Hyacinth and myself went for a walk around town; Cherbourg is quite a pleasant place for a Port. There was the inevitable booze cruise hypermarket which was already doing a roaring trade but further in there are some lovely squares with an outdoor market in one that has all the glorious French food and wine for sale. Cheeses to die for, oysters, mussels, and wine at 50 pence a bottle that sold for £3 in Britain.

However, what we should remember when thinking that France is cheap is that they, like most of the rest of Europe, pay far more tax than we do in Britain. (In fact Britain has virtually the lowest total tax take as a proportion of GDP in Europe. The only countries that pay less are Italy and Southern Ireland). French income tax rates are about 60%. For that they get superb public services; if you need an operation in France you get one within three days; the trains are efficient and cheap; schools have plenty of money to educate. Everyone also gets at least 9 weeks paid holiday a year. The French attitude to life is that we are not just put on this earth to work all the time. Life should be enjoyed with leisure time for everyone.

I remember being told in the 1970s that the new technology of computers would create a leisure society. We could all have much more holiday, as computers would do a lot of the jobs for us. The idea was that it would work like this. A team of 10 accountants take five days to add up the figures for a company's account. A computer is introduced that can do the job in 10 seconds. Some of those five days could be given to the accountants as extra holiday perhaps finishing work at lunchtime on a Friday.

The same idea could be applied to those paint spraying cars in factories or any other of the thousands of jobs that are now done by computer. We could all work shorter hours and therefore create more jobs and have less unemployment. The dream did not seem to happen in Britain; we have the longest working hours and shortest holidays of any country in Europe.

Anyway after that rant I will return to Cherbourg. The market was fun; we purchased lots of smelly cheese and cheap wine. We then wandered back in the general direction of the hotel.

We went into our rooms - en suite but fairly small. We unpacked the huge suitcase and filled up two wardrobes, one and half for Hyacinth, half for me! Hyacinth settled down to watch the television (she doesn't do running, she also doesn't speak French so the TV must have been interesting!) and I met the rest of the hash outside the hotel. We were directed by Loading Bay and Poubelle to a bus stop on the main road.

6: Cherbourg

We went about 4 miles down the road to a lovely town called Auderville set at the bottom of a small wooded hill. The run started from outside the town hall (Le Mairie) and went straight up the hill through the woods. The scenery was very French, the sun was shining, the happy cries of On On! reverberated through the woods and the locals looked on in amazement at these mad Englishmen. I found myself at the front of the pack due to a lucky line out.

I came out of the woods and ran across the road to a stream with a small bridge across to a sort of wooden structure with a seat inside. It was incredibly peaceful inside; the sound of the stream was muted through the wood of the building. I was enjoying sitting and relaxing in this idyllic spot. Then the rest of the hash turned up and decided to have a competition to see how many hashers we could squeeze in to a small wooden structure. I was at the back and was crushed into the wall; we achieved a score of eighteen people in a structure designed for four. We even managed to close the door. I wondered if we would get a place in the Guinness Book of Records.

We continued round in a large circle across hills, dales and through fields and eventually returned to the town hall by a devious back route. It was probably only about a four mile run but it felt longer. We got the bus back to the hotel, showered, and went to the bar de la Pays just down the road. Mr Magoo our GM (a fluent French speaker) had tried his best to explain to the bar owner what hashing was all about, how we would come in, sing some songs and drink some beer. We had a phonetic French version of 'He's a hasher, he's a blue' which enabled us to sing in French without worrying about pronunciation.

Nearly everyone got a down down for offences real and imaginary. The owner and the locals really thought it was great fun and even joined in the singing. They were not quite as impressed as we flew Cooperman around the bar. This involved six hashers picking him up; he takes up the classic superman pose and flies around the room. Unfortunately he was almost dropped onto one of the tables, knocking over several glasses of beer. He refused to do any more flying in French air space!

Most of us went back to the hotel for some sleep. Mongrel and Poor Sod stayed in the bar, Mongrel was attempting to drink a gin and tonic using chopsticks for some reason. She practised her appalling French on anyone who would listen. She tended to speak a mixture of French and English words but made up for the English words by saying them with a French accent. The result was a kind of hybrid that neither an English speaker nor a French speaker could understand! She managed to tell the bar's owner that she loved him when she meant to say she loved his bar! His wife was not happy about this at all.

After a few hours sleep back at the hotel Du Louvre we met up to go for the evening meal. The hash split into separate groups and about ten of us decided to go to the La Taverna restaurant just down the road. Snowman was not keen on spending much money on grub but we eventually convinced him to give it a go. Our group was directed upstairs and we got the top floor to ourselves. The waitress was efficient and patient with our inability to read French. Most of us decided to go for a moules starter and steak or chicken to follow. Cooperman was hungry so he ordered a moules starter and an extra large steak with French fries.

The moules were spectacular; a white wine and garlic sauce made every mouthful a gastronomic experience. We each had a ceramic pot full of them - about the size of a dustbin. They went on forever with sticks of bread to mop up the sauce. Snowman was instantly a convert to French cuisine - he had never tasted anything like it. We had several bottles of wine to wash it all down and then the traditional long break before the next course. We needed it as we were all stuffed with crustacean bi-valves.

After a good half an hour the steaks started to arrive. I was glad I had gone for the small one as it was about 32 ounces and covered the entire surface of a large dinner plate. When Cooperman's large one arrived it was astonishing; it didn't arrive on a plate, it was served on a wooden platter about the size of a small raft. The chips just kept on coming and Coops was determined to eat it all. The cream and brandy sauce was incredibly rich but he eventually managed to plough his way through this mountain of food. He sat slumped at the table totally immobile and turning green. 'Fancy a pudding Coops?' asked a rather insensitive Fracas! 'Sod off!' came the reply.

We slowly made our way down stairs and there was a queue for the ladies loo. One of the female hashers decided she wasn't going to wait and so went into the gents and used a urinal. How she managed to pee into a urinal without a penis, will, I hope, remain an anatomical mystery to me to the rest of my days.

6: Cherbourg

Across the road there was a bar and mini brewery. It actually had the stainless steel fermenting vessels along the back wall. Various pipes gurgled and the smell of yeast pervaded the whole place. The beer was wicked - a terrific flavour and of course being English we ordered a Grand beer (by the pint) not the piddly little thirds that the French drink. Snowman ordered a giraffe of beer for the table - it is a huge tube with a tap at the bottom containing about eight pints of beer.

After my second pint I thought the world was feeling quite good and I had a look at the menu to find out about the beer. I was astonished to find that the weakest beer on the menu was 6% by volume. I will say that again! The weakest beer was 6% by volume and they went up to about 14%! (Like drinking a strong wine by the pint) The stuff we were drinking was 7%! No wonder they drink it in the little piddly glasses with lots of froth!

We staggered out of the bar and headed for the seafront harbour area. There was some kind of festival on and there was a stage set up with a band playing some French rock and roll numbers. There were lots of small marquees set up around the edge of the harbour wall selling all kinds of arty stuff and various designer clothes. The band eventually stopped the raucous row they were making and some kind of circle dance started. This involved moving in a circle and holding little fingers with the person behind and in front of you. The French were very welcoming and helped us all to join in the dance. They were patient when we messed up the steps or went the wrong way and we all spent a fun hour dancing around by the harbour and drinking yet more beer!

At about 1 am we all decided to head back to the hotel and we managed to collapse into bed and sleep solidly until 6 am when Cooperman came knocking at the door. 'What the hell are you doing banging on our door at this time' I asked in a fairly calm voice, considering I had only been asleep 5 hours. 'Oh I thought this was Steve's room. We are laying the hangover run together,' he said and wandered off down the corridor banging on random doors. I went back to bed and slept solidly to lunch time, missing Cooperman's hangover run.

We went back to the bar de Pays for down downs. Ermintrude (she wears lots of eye makeup and always runs dressed immaculately) got one for discovering the French porn on the television the night before. Mongrel got one for telling the owner of the bar she loved him and Cooperman got one for waking half the hash up at an unearthly hour.

We returned to La Taverna restaurant and enjoyed soupe de poisson (fish soup), absolutely gorgeous' with a bit of bread and cheese floating on top, followed by chicken in white wine sauce boiled potatoes and crunchy vegetables that had only dipped their toe in the boiling water. That is the way to cook vegetables not boiled until they go a shade of grey and all the vitamins have been drowned. The cheese board followed; I did some serious damage to the Camembert and Hyacinth destroyed the Brie. The price of this meal, with two glasses of wine, was about £4.50 each - incredible value.

It was time to bid a fond farewell to Cherbourg so we got a taxi back to the ferry terminal. The return journey was made on the catamaran service which only takes about 3 hours to get to Portsmouth. It's convenient but a bit like flying on an aircraft; there is a little bar and café to eat in but no real restaurants, no cinema and definitely no swimming pool. The deck area is also very limited, just a small outdoor space at the back with no real view. The shop, however, had a good supply of newspapers and books so I immersed myself in the universe of Terry Pratchett - his disc world books are a work of genius. We got back to the Island at about 12.30 am.

I have reproduced below Mongrel's write-up on the trip. It is Mongrelese, a combination of French, English and dog. It cannot be understood by anyone.

Francais-Je suis facile!
La post card du la Hash journe a la Francais

La Trip wast tres bon. Vingt du uns arrive dans Cherbourg. Monsuer Mark ave une grand vallaise – avec tres clothes. Il arrive a la bar de paix et depart encore –alors –il arrive ancore dans neveux clothes. En samdi nous (moi et cinq mon ami) avoncroque madame pour petite dejiner. Tres bon et la waiter, Jai t em im. Apres petite de-junne nous went jogging- cest magnifique – et la sol ce wast oeuf. Les gluey-gleuys a la bar de paixwere tes jollie. Apres nous all journe dans alternique directions por dejuner. En la après di, only douze de us went jogging. C'est bon trail dans la rues de Cherboug. Apres nous allez a la bar de paix encore – jai voir mon amis ici, madame et Alain- a tres bon homme. J'ai purchase un beir avec mon amies et les hashers est all ah encore gluey- glueys. Jaitres

6: Cherbourg

miserable du parle au revoir mon amis a la bar. Cest vie. Sonau faire ann – alors nous manage un bon luncheon mais madam Dima est pisse dans la eurinels – jai wast tres shocked. Allomous returnee UK un tres bon weekend-mon at est off to steve.

Ecrivee par Mongrel (pendant la retour a l;Anglaterre)

www.iwhhh.org.uk

Chapter 7

Alverstone Run

The weathermen were warning of severe conditions in the coming week - icy Northerly winds and a good chance of snow. 'Enjoy the weekend!' they said, as this was the last chance of good weather for at least a week. I grabbed my running gear and set off for Alverstone Garden village. I drove out of Ryde towards Brading, a village about 3 miles away with a quaint church and a small wax works museum. This is open 365 days a year according to the sign, although personally I have never tried to go in there on Christmas day! I can highly recommend it; though not as large as Madame Tussauds in London it is much more intimate and interesting, and there is never a queue that takes 3 hours to negotiate.

It is really one big house and lots of little houses all knocked together so there are strange winding corridors that all have wax models at the end. You walk up steps, down inclines and even come out into a central courtyard with a fountain. There are plenty of historic characters such as Queen Victoria, beautifully displayed, together with characters of local interest such as Valentine Gray, the child chimney sweep, who was starved and then beaten to death by the man who owned him. The ensuing court case was one of the main reasons that children were stopped from going up chimneys in the last century.

I passed out of the town, following the main road to Sandown. As I came to the traffic lights I turned right and followed a winding narrow road, called Alverstone quiet road, through the countryside to Alverstone village. This is a beautiful little village with a church and local corner shop. There are notices on the church board inviting all residents to a cheese and wine get together; a whist drive; or a cup of tea with Miss Marple!

However, there is no pub in the village. In the 1800s Lord Alvestone, the owner of all the land around, had a drunken son (sorry, alcoholic son, he was too posh to be a drunkard) who was always getting into trouble after having one too many at the local hostelry. He eventually became so exasperated with his son that he forced him to live within the boundaries of Alvestone village and had all the pubs closed down.

The On On! was down a little footpath to the right, across some fields, and then up a steep incline which brought us to the top of a hill overlooking the village. Cooperman explained how the village had been very small and just outside the boundary was the municipal tip. Once the tip was full it was covered over; and during the 1960s there was a huge housing boom that produced the extension to the village we could see today. It was an arresting view, crisp blue sky over green fields down to a typical old English village. I found it impossible to imagine why anyone would put a tip in such a place. However, there was no sign at all that there ever had been a tip, so the reclamation job had been very successful.

We continued over the top of the hill and on towards Queens Bough and Borthwood copse which has a clearing in it. There are lots of mature oaks, elms and silver birch trees; all with plenty of space around them. Some were twisted over by the prevailing winds and the ground was covered in dead leaves. The sky was absolutely cloudless; that sort of blue you only get before a big storm is coming. When we stopped it was completely silent. I thought it looked like Lothlorien from the Lord of the Rings. Malcolm (hash name Bilbo) said he felt very at home there. It was worth getting out of bed early on a Sunday morning just to see such a sight.

We climbed up the hill out of the clearing and were rewarded by a view of Sandown bay and the white face of Culver cliff. Flossie turned to run on and was attacked by a tree; well, she ran into a little one and did some serious damage: it didn't do her much good either.

7: Alverstone Run

There was not much sympathy from the hash, just sarcastic comments about what dodgy buggers trees are, always jumping out on people! Tio Pepe was doing some sort of bizarre exercise at the check, that involved lying on the floor and putting his legs around trees. 'My God!' said one of the passing fit runners. 'What have the hash got against trees? Flossing is trying to beat them up and Tio is trying to shag them.'

We carried on for about a mile passing some obnoxious equestrians who seemed to think they owned the public footpath. "I say, how many more of you are there? This is our farm, you know." 'Yes, and this is a public footpath that has been here long before your farm was built. If you don't want people walking through your farm yard why did you buy a farm with a public footpath running through the middle of it?' said a rather pissed off hasher.

We got back on the main road and continued into another wood, then up yet another hill. At the top we came to Hill Farm just around the back of Newchurch (walk down the footpath that goes past the graveyard at Newchurch town church; keep going for 20 minutes and you are there). There is the most wonderful pigsty on the left where free range porkers wander around. They were all inside the little house today and we could not see them. However, in the summer they are always outside and are very friendly. The pigs put their front trotters on the fence and say hello to any passer-by. the piglets run around squealing and looking very cute. The owners here were completely different as the hash passed through, even asking us if we needed directions and saying don't worry about the gate we will close it when you are all through.

It was all downhill from there onwards; we passed the sand quarry where the sound of motorbikes racing about could be heard. Then on to the old railway line and the watermill; a grand old house on the bank of a man-made lake. Cooperman said that there used to be a railway stop there in the sixties and people would get the train to this idyllic spot and hire a rowing boat for the afternoon. Post Beeching all that remains of the track now is the public footpath that we are running on and occasional sleepers, used as part of the safety rails on bridges.

We got back to the cars, changed out of our running gear and headed for the comical pub at Sandown. It is a typical town pub in the High Street all wooden beams and tables. The only complaint is that they do not serve food on a Sunday; after a run I am always famished but had to make do with a packet of peanuts.

Several down downs followed; Cooperman got one for doing an excellent job as the hare. 'It was a terrific run through some beautiful countryside' said the RA. Flossie and Tio Pepe got one each for tree abuse, Snowman and Mudflap for enthusiastic running (or something like that!). One or two Scb's (short cutting bastards) got their come-uppance.

I drove back to Ryde in high spirits with lots of post exercise endorphins running through my brain. I am convinced that anyone who has not tried hashing would have been converted if they had been on that run.

CHAPTER 8

EUROHASH AARHUS

It was a bright clear sunny morning in August. I picked up Interloper at 8am and we made our way to the ferry port at Fishbourne. We were worried about the time as the ship left from Harwich at 4pm and we had no idea how long it would take to drive up to London around the M25 (Chris Rea's road to hell) and down the A12 To Harwich.

As it was we managed to catch the 8.30 ferry from the Isle of Wight and we arrived in Harwich at about noon - this gave us plenty of time to explore which turned out to be a mistake. The weather on the East coast had taken a turn for the worse. The leaden grey sky reflected our mood as we walked the streets of this complete dump. We searched in vain for a red warning triangle; there was no Halfords to be found and the only motoring shop had sold out. The only chain visible on the high street was Woolworths. There was not a decent pub anywhere; the one at the end of the high street would only feel safe if you were in riot gear! There was a café and snooker hall combined called 'Gods Waiting Room' (or something like that) where people go to drink tea and die.

We searched the seafront looking for refreshment and found a decaying 1950s hotel with 2 stars. As far as we could see this was the best place in town. I asked the Essex girl behind the bar for a pot of

Earl Grey. She responded with a look of baffled bewilderment. "Yu wot?" she responded, clearly Earl Grey was off the menu. 'What sort of tea do you serve?' I asked. 'This stuff in bags!' she responded. I took my bag of PG tips and placed it in the lukewarm water she gave me in a plastic cup.

We decided to spend the last hour waiting at the ferry port. There, standing resplendent in its gleaming white paint, was our boat. We couldn't wait to get on board and use the sauna and swimming pool advertised in the brochure. The food also looked superb – quite unusual for a ferry.

When we found our cabin we were in a good mood. We watched Harwich slip by from the window and really started to relax. However, we searched the ship from top to bottom trying to find the swimming pool and sauna. On referring back to the brochure we realised they had both disappeared into a colon (: not available on all sailings, it said).

The announcement system informed us of the evening's entertainment. There was a Transylvanian band, unusual, Bingo (wow!) a disco and a Zauberer (German for magician). The food I must say was excellent' if a little expensive' and after our meal we went into the Navigator bar (good name for a bar! I really felt at home), for a gentle beer or two.

At 7pm it was time for the bingo, so we stayed in the bar and lots of others joined us trying to avoid this nauseous activity. At 8pm we moved down the boat to the nightclub where the Zauberer was about to start his magic show. There were lots of Germans looking very keen 'Ya Ya bring on the Zauberer' they said 'Oh yes the Zauberer terrific' (Interloper can speak German). The Zauberer appeared and did some basic magic- more in the style of Tommy Cooper than Harry Potter. The audience were ecstatic at his performance and cheered, calling for more. Interloper and I really couldn't see what was so impressive.

Interloper, I think, summed it all up very well when he said rather loudly 'I wish he would bloody well make himself disappear. If you do not answer our questions, you will be forced to watch the Zauberer' (in a rather good German accent). The Transylvanian band looked as though they had spent the previous night at Dracula's castle. The singer looked white as a sheet and the bass player moved

8: Eurohash Aarhus

in a minimalist fashion with his whole body rigid and only his fingers moving slowly over the strings.

Arriving the next day at Cruxhaven we drove down a very slow B road to Hamburg. The small towns we passed through were pleasant enough with a homely feel and the sun was shining - even thoughts of the Zarberer could not dampen our spirits. We were heading for Hamburg, city of a thousand surprises, the first of which was that there is bugger all there!

We could not find a Beer Keller anywhere; all we wanted was a bit of German quaffing and singing with fat men in short trousers. It was not to be - there was no genuine German beer to be found and the only fat people around were the two of us. The whole of Hamburg felt like Coventry; the same sort of 1970s architecture. Thinking about it there is probably a reason for that!

We ended up in one of the many Irish bars that seem to have replaced the Beer Kellers - lots of Guinness but no Steins of frothy German beer. Looking for food we were directed by the barmaid to an Italian restaurant across the road. We enjoyed a repast of Mozzarella salad followed by seafood spaghetti and four small beers each. The cost of this very average meal was £42 each, basically extortion. Sometimes God is on your side and things go right. We got the bill and realised their till had made a mistake - it had only added up the cost of one meal. We paid in cash and asked where the cash point was to get some more money out. They directed us down the road and as we were about to take the money out a waiter came jogging out of the restaurant looking for us, I know it was a little naughty but we disappeared around the corner - the meal really was not worth what they wanted to charge.

The next day we took the Autobahn to Denmark, an excellent road with no tolls even on the huge bridges and long tunnels. One of the tunnels was under the Elba and seemed twice as long as the Dartford tunnel but it did not cost us a Euro. The road had two lanes and the inside lane only did 50 miles per hour. I went into the outside lane and cruised along at 80. However, there was a flashing BMW in my mirror within seconds. I accelerated to the Rovers top speed of 105 miles per hour and there were still lots of cars flashing to get past. How fast do you have to go! We did the 200 miles to Aarhus in what felt like 10 minutes. These Autobahns are very quick!

Arriving in Aarhus something happened. Every second woman was beautiful, every 5th woman was gorgeous and every 10th woman was a model. It was very distracting - I almost had 3 accidents (car). I do not know what causes this phenomenon - it is either the gene pool or Aarhus is the original location of the Stepford wives.

We went to our campsite via the container port (Navigator!) and set up our tents. The camp site was about 2 miles outside Aarhus at a place called Bloomhaven. There was a wood and beach in front of our tents with a super view across to Sweden. The facilities included a Solarium and the inevitable Sauna.

The traditional start of all big hash events is a run for charity in a red dress. We donned our red dresses and caught the bus back into town. The run was due to start from the Naxos bar back in Aarhus. This was apparently a leading gay bar. I couldn't help feeling it was not a good idea to enter a gay bar wearing a red dress. However, there was nothing to worry about as there were about 120 hashers already inside wearing the red.

We walked down the steps of the Naxos to the basement bar. This was tastefully decorated with oak beams across the roof; mosaic type pictures of Greek gods and lots of old world ornaments along the sides. It was heaving with red clad hashers attempting to register and buy beer. I must say the girl in front looked very nice with ponytails and fishnets, very neat figure I thought. Well, that was until she turned round and I realised it was a bearded Twonk dressed up by Mongrel to look like a girly girl. They even had matching handbags! I need help! Fancying Twonk in a gay bar is dangerous!

The run started and we headed down the main road and on into the centre of town. Aarhus really is a beautifully elegant city with a river running through the middle and modern glass sided buildings lining the side. These are a combination of shops and riverside bars with restaurants in between. I do not understand why more of this café culture is not prevalent in Britain. I have always been told that the weather is the problem in England - outdoor cafes only work in a hot climate. Well, it seems to work in Aarhus and it is on the same latitude as Aberdeen!

We must have run about 600 yards when we stopped outside the Women's Museum. No one seemed to know what this contained. I got slapped for suggesting that if it contained antique women then we

8: Eurohash Aarhus

have plenty of exhibits on the hash. Several hashers did get invited inside, including Mongrel and Snowman. They took lots of photographs from the balcony producing some stunning aerial shots of red clad hashers.

Continuing into town the front-runners were some American guys who decided to give everyone they met a hug. They were huge, at least 6 foot 5 inches tall. They ran up to several of the most gorgeous looking women saying everyone needs a hug. Most reacted well and gave them a hug back. A group of skinheads outside one of the bars tried to take the piss out of these guys wearing red dresses so three of them went up and kissed their bald patches. They started to look aggressive but then backed off as a hundred red dresses appeared around the corner. The poor manager of the local Macdonalds thought his time had come as six huge hashers gave him a hug and a kiss on their way past.

We arrived at a long cobbled street in the old town for a beer stop. This turned out to be rather unusual. One of the Arhus hashers produced a pram of wicked spirits rather than the usual trip inside a pub. The pram contained Russian Vodkas and what tasted like Absinthe although I am sure it wasn't, as judging by the quantities some people put away they would have been having hallucinations. We managed to block the old town off completely, so hashers had to be cleared out of the way when bicycles or cars wanted to come through. A guide wearing helicopter rotor blades on his head and no shorts, would lead them through the middle of the pack that parted like the Red Sea.

We ran on through he town centre shouting On On! and giving lots of entertainment to the locals who did not seem to have seen anything like it before. (We made front page of the local paper the next day!) As we arrived back at the river Slipshod informed us that he had got us all a beer in at the Cockney pub just up the road. Snowman, Slipshod, Cooperman, Interloper and myself all sneaked away from the run and went back to the pub. This turned out to be a very good move. The beer was superb; London Pride and Abbots kept as though it was yards from the brewery, not a thousand miles away. The host, Craig Monk, was incredibly welcoming; we were all still in red dresses and he didn't bat an eyelid.

When is it due?' I was asked by one of the girls sitting in the corner (when I went to a charity shop in Ryde to buy my red dress - the only one I could find that would fit was an old maternity outfit). I was standing by the front entrance resplendent in red maternity wear and clearly I looked very pregnant. 'Well is it due next month?' 'You must be at least nine months gone.' I felt this was a little harsh as I had lost a stone in weight since the start of the summer holiday. Like most young Danish women they were beautiful and after talking to them we found them interesting and intelligent. One was doing a Master's degree in French, another was just finishing her PHD on English literature, Interloper had a competition with her to see who could quote the most Macbeth to each other. Interestingly they told us that they preferred to speak in English rather than in Danish - they found that English was a more expressive language and had a larger vocabulary. (I wish someone would tell the French this!) Craig the barman kept telling us how wonderful it was to have such a lively crowd in and how the place actually felt like a genuine cockney pub for the first time he could remember.

After several hours and more than several pints of Abbots ale some of us decided it was time to call it a night. Slipshod found the pub exit assisted by his faithful companion Snowman. Interloper and I got a taxi that parked within two steps of the door. This was fortunate, as I probably could not have walked any further!

We awoke at our campsite the next morning feeling a little worse for wear. We wandered down to the shower block, which was spotlessly clean and superbly maintained. It even had musak gently playing in the background; I presume this was to prevent anyone hearing any plopping sounds from the cubicle next door (they think of everything the Danish).

Leaving the camp site at about noon we set off for the motorway (route 45) back South to a place called Ry. This is pronounced Roo and is about 20 miles south of Arhus; it is a small spotless town surrounded by rivers woods and lakes, a paradise for backpackers and hashers alike. Ry is really just a big village but is served by a superb railway service. Denmark did not close down all its non-commercial railways in the sixties; they are run as a public service, which reduces the traffic on the roads and helps prevent pollution.

When we arrived at the hash camp site they were still building it, putting up the roof between the building and the marquee. The site was a large youth hostel, with camping at the back. It was situated across the road from a crystal clear lake; beach and small wooded

8: Eurohash Aarhus

area. The registration queue was long and noisy; Windsock was creating most of the noise. He demanded, in not unreasonable terms, to know why the process was taking so long. Statements like 'It's really bloody boring waiting here,' and 'Get on with it you wankers!' were some of his more polite statements!

Interloper and I gave up on the queue and went out to put up the tents. I always get a pleasant tingle of anticipation when putting up a tent at the start of a camping trip - there is a positive atmosphere, with everyone helping each other out. One of the Scottish contingent managed to explode his inflatable bed. He connected it up to an electric car pump and just forgot about it while looking for beer. The bang it made was like a small nuclear device and a number of hashers leaped into the air including me.

We went inside for dinner and enjoyed a spicy chilli; there was plenty of it in a variety of temperatures and a vegetarian option. The beer was Carlsberg, which pleased me no end but disappointed Snowman and many others from the IOW Real Ale Hash Society. We were a little subdued that evening due to the vast amount of alcohol consumed the previous night. Only Mongrel and Cooperman seemed unaffected. Mongrel ran around like an untrained Rottwieler frightening the French contingent. She had one of them cornered in the bar and Snowman advised him to run for his life! Cooperman, went on the torchlight run - the guy is indestructible. However it is good to see at least one of the IOW hash taking the running seriously. He enjoyed every hilly mile and described in detail the skinny-dipping in the lake at the end.

The next morning I was awoken by the sound of bagpipes at the unearthly hour of 9am. Some Scottish bastards decided we all needed waking up and went round the tents playing Scotland the Git or something! I got out of my sleeping bag, crawled out of my tent and shouted abuse. Sadly the racket drowned all this out and they marched on regardless.

I got up and went in search of a shower. This proved difficult as there were huge queues outside all the shower rooms. I was about to give up when I remembered that there were some showers across the road on the beach. They faced towards the woods so no one would notice me. I went across, undressed and got into the shower; it was freezing cold but very refreshing. I had only been in there for 30 seconds when a gorgeous female Danish hasher with deep red hair walked around the corner. She asked me if the shower next to me was free. "Yes I think so", I spluttered from the cold and the fact that she was taking her clothes off. She got into the shower next door and we talked about hashing. She was apparently Danish but lived abroad at the moment. I told her that my hash name was Navigator because I always get lost. I asked her what she was called. 'Red Beaver she replied.' 'Oh why is that' I asked and realised it was a really stupid question!

It seemed that the place was turning into Euston Station. A guy with the same shower idea as me appeared around the corner and then apologised to Red Beaver when he saw her in the shower. 'It's all right,' she said 'It's a free country!' Then Snowman appeared with his camera so I rapidly got dressed and told him to bugger off. Red Beaver just laughed and said he was too late.

I got back to the campsite and sorted out a packed lunch to take with me on the run. Interloper was already sorted out and as he was a virgin, I agreed to accompany him on the short run (his first ever hash run was on the Euro-hash! This has got to be some sort of record). I had convinced Interloper to come along by telling him how much running was involved, how he would get fit and lose lots of weight by doing this highly athletic activity.

We boarded the bus for the short run: Large Roman Member and Unfortunate Things Occur were the hares. We drove out to the town of Skanderborg; the coach stopped just by the sports field where some big Danish football match was taking place. There must have been as many as six people in the watching crowd.

We walked around the field and got to the edge of the woods. We were then informed of the usual rules - that three blobs of flour was on, line out should be obeyed and that the symbol for a fish hook was the usual hook shape. Higgins showed us a new symbol, a circle with a large N in the middle. This was called a naughty check. We were instructed to stand in the middle - bend over with hands on knees. We must then allow the person behind us to spank us on the bottom. The second person then replaces the first person and the third one spanks them etc; the last person was asked to spank himself or herself! Probably the best place to be!

We then walked slowly through the woods and I was starting to wonder when the actual running would begin. I did tell Interloper that I thought it was a little slow getting started and suggested that we run

8: Eurohash Aarhus

through the pack to encourage them. I really did want some exercise. Well, we started running and were singularly ignored by the hashers. Commercial Whale asked Interloper why he was running. Interloper replied that he thought that running was what hashing was all about. "No no no" he said in a deep Scottish accent. 'Sensible hashers don't run Interloper, in fact, on this run, you can be given a down down for running; I should be careful if I were you.' A few minutes later Commercial Whale was up and running fast 'Why are you running now?' Interloper asked. 'Och there is a beer stop coming up soon! You have to run for that!'

Interloper became a little sarcastic after this incident and started chanting On On in a very cynical manner. He did not seem to believe that hashing involved any running at all and what we did was drink and go for a stroll in the woods. He was not even convinced when I told him the run was atypical, and that on the Isle of Wight we always do at least four miles of running, sometimes much more. I am still trying to persuade him to come on an Island run and see what real hashing is all about.

On the way to the down downs we met Pure Genius one of the Guernsey girls. She got her hash name because she has a medical condition that requires her to have Guinness on prescription it is even delivered to her house. That really is Pure Genius.

The down downs were at the coach just by the stadium and a residential area. They went on for a very long time with some rather dodgy new songs. I felt sorry for the local residents after the fourth verse of Hashy Birthday F*** you! The curtains were all twitching by this point. We also had Chinese fire alarms (everyone runs from one side of the circle to the other, very rapidly) and Rastafarian fire alarms (everyone strolls across the circle going "yeh mon").

There were down downs for nearly everyone including Interloper for being a virgin on the Euro hash. A New Zealand girl got one for having travelled the furthest of anyone there. One of the Americans seemed to think China was further away than New Zealand. Clearly she had the same Geography teacher as George Bush!

We returned to the campsite in glorious sunshine. The water of the lake looked very tempting, particularly as there was a hash raft floating just off shore, with lots of hashers on board drinking beer. This looked like an excellent idea so a crowd of us dived into the water: some wearing clothes, some going for the skinny-dipping option. We arrived at the raft and were greeted by a very organised Candyfloss who asked if we all wanted a beer. I was most impressed as he took the caps off the bottles and stored them inside his trunks preventing any pollution of the crystal clear lake.

The sun was shining; the water was cool and refreshing. As soon as the beer ran out the refrain of "more beer, more beer, more beer" (to the tune of amazing grace) would drift out from the raft and some helpful hasher would go and get a case. This song was interspersed with 'Get your tits out for the boys' (to the tune of Bread of Heaven from Guide Me Oh Thou Great Redeemer). As more beer was drunk so less clothing was worn. Various people swapped swimming trunks for swimming costumes. However, the girls' swimming costumes were usually far too small for the boys to wear and the boys' shorts kept slipping off the girls so there were some interesting sights. (Not for the faint hearted).

The boat was getting a little overcrowded and kept drifting in to shore. Windsock got out and pushed the anchor in the ground several times but to little avail. Then Fat Bastard swam out and as he got aboard, the raft converted into a submarine. It was just like a James Bond movie! I had to hold my beer above my head to stop the water getting in, as we slowly sank to the bottom of the lake. It was a terrific way to spend an afternoon, drinking beer, getting a tan and enjoying the company of lively, fun loving hashers.

At 6pm it was time to get dinner. There was a choice of several different meats, baked potatoes and a variety of salads. You could absolutely stuff yourself and still have plenty more to eat - the food just kept coming. Whoever organised the catering at Eurohash did a very good job.

The band started about 7.30 and they were pretty good, playing all the well-known songs you love to bop along to, mainly golden oldies. The cabarets had the usual mix of performances from excellent to diabolical. There was a non-sexist wet T shirt competition for boys and girls. There were lots of entries but it was won by the Gurnsey girls who all entered as one contestant.

Windsock won the Miss Eurohash competition and his wife Topps won the Mr Eurohash competition. Windsock also did an impromptu

8: Eurohash Aarhus

cabaret involving tearing up paper, that no one seemed to understand, but cheered all the same.

I was really enjoying the excellent red wine; it was in a bottle (rather than the usual hash box) and was of a fairly good quality. Mongrel had the "superb" idea of getting a bottle of wine from them rather than going back every few minutes to top up our glasses. Interloper, Mongrel and I then went on to drink a third of a bottle each in about ten minutes. So we got another bottle, after three more bottles the world was becoming hazy and we were all talking bollocks (no change there then!).

It was about this time that they announced the naked hash,* the Full Monty played and people took their clothes off all over the dance floor. Clothes were laid neatly outside the marquee so they could be found easily afterwards and there was a run around the campsite.

This ended in a dark area of the field where there were the down downs. Large Roman Member was the RA and walked into the centre wearing clothes: this was frowned upon so he quickly removed them. It was noticed that several young American ladies were also in the circle fully clothed. They were gallantly assisted in undressing by several helpful Gentlemen! There then followed down downs for lots of imaginary offences and a naughty check was set up for anyone in the circle without their partners.

They returned to the brightly lit area where the clothes had all been neatly placed in separate piles only to find that some helpful hashers had mixed them all up into one great big bundle! It took some of them 15 minutes to find even one item of clothing.

The next day I awoke with my mouth feeling like the bottom of a birdcage. There was a large contingent of gnomes inside my head trying to get out using sledgehammers.

It was 11.am and I staggered to the car to find the aspirin, only to meet Interloper on the way who looked bright as a button (bastard!). His powers of recovery are legendary - he had been up for ages and felt fine. I very slowly took my tent down and watched the hangover runners setting off towards the buses.

All big hash events seem to have a naked run at midnight, I have yet to find out where this tradition originates.

Interloper and I drove into Ry where we found a hotel that was serving lunch. I picked my way through a tuna salad while Interloper tucked into steak and chips. We decided to return to Arhus for the night and so drove the 20 miles back up the road. We spent the day recovering on the beach and went for a swim. There was a pub-crawl in the evening but we felt too exhausted to go and so got an Indian takeaway. It was probably the worst Indian I have ever tasted - it had no hot flavour at all and was just chicken in slightly spicy gravy.

I don't know what it is about mainland Europe but they don't seem to have a clue how to make curry. I even tried a curry in France, the home normally of gastronomic delights, only to be very disappointed. When I lived in Bradford I was told that they served the best curries in Europe; I did not believe it at the time but now I feel they are probably right.

It was actually a shame that we missed the pub-crawl as Mongrel told me what happened later. After the hangover runs, lots of hashers had returned to the lake for more beers and a swim. Twonk had swapped swimming costumes with one of the girls. She was wearing black shorts and he was wearing a pink swimming costume that was far too small for him and left nothing to the imagination. Mongrel then called him out of the lake and told him she had arranged a lift into Arhus but that he must come straight away. He rushed to get into the car and it wasn't until he was 2 miles down the road that he realised what he was wearing.

No one was going to turn round so he arrived in Arhus wearing a very tight fitting pink swimsuit and nothing else. They were heading for the Naxos bar but unfortunately this involved walking past the very plush restaurants along the riverfront. Huge crowds of people were dining on the pavements enjoying the warm night air. Twonk said to Mongrel "I cannot walk along there dressed like this." Mongrel did her girly girl impression and said, 'Don't worry, just walk with your head up smiling, hold my hand and walk slowly past with dignity.'

Apparently there were some astonished expressions as he walked past; at one table all conversation stopped and jaws dropped as he went by. He felt very relieved when he arrived outside the Naxos and could join a crowd of hashers inside where he would not stand out.

However, this was not to be. The Naxos bar was closed and the rest of the hash had gone to another pub. The pub was at the other end of

8: Eurohash Aarhus

the river and Twonk would have to walk past again! He was not happy but plucked up his courage, grabbed Mongrel's hand and walked back again. As he passed the first table a huge cheer went up from the diners and a Mexican wave followed him from table to table as he walked down the river.

They arrived at the pub and went in for a beer then moved on to the next pub, walking down a very narrow road. At this point they blocked the traffic and there was a convertible red Ferrari trying to get through, honking his horn. When he stopped Twonk jumped into the back seat and sat there looking sexy while others took photographs. 'Get out of my car!' said the Ferrari's owner who had no sense of humour. 'Get out of my car now!' Twonk tried to get out but couldn't get himself over the door. The car's owner was so angry he didn't even notice the Guernsey girls sitting on his bumper and smiling into the camera lens.

Interloper and I got up early and started the drive back. The countryside along the motorway is fairly tedious; quite flat, and the only real features are the numerous wind farms that blot the landscape at regular intervals. Huge modern turbines produce electricity without pollution, or using up any fuel. What a great idea! However I feel it would be an even better idea if they were all placed offshore.

Three hours later we were passing by Hamburg and then followed the M22 round towards Cruxhaven. We decided this would be a faster route, even though it was longer in terms of miles travelled. We went off the Autobarn at a place called Bremerhaven and found a hotel for the night. The hotel was very cheap and cheerful but only served sausages and sauerkraut, neither of which we fancied. However, the lager was the genuine German item; frothy and strong with no chemical additives.

We did not know exactly what the town had to offer, beer, food or entertainment wise, so Interloper used his best German to ask the owner where there was to go in town. He was informed that we were at the seaside and that there was nothing down the road except the sea front. He also told Interloper that we would not find any prostitutes in town. Interloper told him we were not looking for that kind of entertainment and renamed him the Shizer Mit Ze Brill (SHIT WITH THE GLASSES). We decided we were definitely not going to eat in his bar and would even forgo another beer. We wandered down to the front and found that the place was a sailing centre with a small river running along the sea front behind a dyke.

There was a restaurant overlooking the front but we couldn't spot any prostitutes. We went in and had a glass or two of lager, although it was not as good as that served by the Shizzer Mit Ze Brille. The food menu was very dull, so we wandered back into town. On the main road out we found a small Greek restaurant that was wonderfully run by friendly, efficient staff - the aromas coming out from the kitchen were gorgeous. The only English the waiter spoke was 'David Beckham' and 'Manchester United' so Interloper ordered. It really was a great meal the starters went on forever with all kinds of small meat dishes, followed by large meat dishes stuffed with vine leaves, olives, Humus and Tazicka.

It was at this point that Interloper discovered he had lost the key to the hotel. This could be an absolute disaster as the last thing we wanted to do was wake up the hotel owner at 1 am. Our relationship with him wasn't exactly off to a good start as we hadn't eaten in his bar and I am sure he heard us talking about 'the shit with the glasses' and realised it was him.

We backtracked over the streets we had walked down searching the gutters and even checked inside the bank at the cash point. No sign of it anywhere! We were just resigning ourselves to becoming the most unpopular people in Bloomhaven when Interloper realised that it may have fallen out in the last bar. He rushed back and found them just locking up. However, on the counter was our hotel key!

The next day we drove down the road to Cruxhaven and arrived with a couple of hours to kill before the ferry left. Cruxhaven is a beautiful little town. Prosperous and well landscaped, the shopping centre is exciting, with lots of coffee bars and a relaxed European feel. The outdoor market had a large collection of cheeses and wonderful wines, plus a variety of reasonably priced clothing. It was easy to kill a couple of hours just enjoying the atmosphere.

Getting onto the ferry took some time in a long boring, queue. However, the Zauberer appeared again and did an excellent job of entertaining the children in the cars, with some close up magic. We explored the ferry again in the hope of finding the swimming pool or the sauna but of course it wasn't available on this ship either.

We had the band, the joys of bingo and the Zauberer all over again. The magician really should stay as a children's entertainer; his tricks

8: Eurohash Aarhus

were simply not impressive enough for an adult audience. We woke up the next day and the tannoy was announcing that all passengers must return their keys unless they were on the mini cruise. I said to Interloper 'What is a mini cruise? Surely they don't cruise over to Harwich and then go back the same day.' I went on a mission to find out; the receptionist explained that "Yes it does happen."

I could not believe this. Some people cruise over from Cruxhaven, enjoy the Bingo, band and the magician then they have five hours to kill in wonderful Harwich. I dread to think the impression the Germans get of Britain if they have come from Cruxhaven and then only see Harwich. They must think Britain is a dreadful place. Once they have finished exploring all Harwich has to offer, they get back on the boat and enjoy the bingo the band and the magician all over again! 'Heaven!'

We returned to the Isle of Wight on the 5pm ferry completely exhausted, but we had had a terrific time. I am booking up immediately for the next Eurohash in Amsterdam. The Dutch hashers include a splif in your goody bag so you get some hash from the Hash! I cannot wait!

Chapter 9

Nash Hash in the Cotswolds

I really felt completely Hashed out after Europe. However, it was only a week later that Hyacinth and I set out for Nash Hash. This was at Westonbirts girls' school, a private institution near Tetbury in the Cotswolds. Hyacinth and I arrived at about 4pm. We drove past acres of fields and eventually arrived at the school. The marquee was dwarfed by the sheer scale of the place. The building is really impressive; a huge mansion built in Italian style, with massive grounds including an Arboretum and Cotswold centre. It was one of those posh boarding schools that only have 'Gals' as pupils; I was amazed that they had rented it out to the hash (Stretch must have been very persuasive). I presumed they did not know what they were letting themselves in for.

The school site was originally an Elizabethan stately home built in 1665 and owned by the Holford family. It was knocked down and rebuilt in Italian style in the 1800s by Peter Holford, the son of the original owner. The gardens are huge and open to the public. It is stated in the brochure that the family made their money out of selling water to London. Apparently the manor house stands on huge underground reservoirs. It was converted to a school in 1928.

We went inside the main entrance hall, a vision of marble with supporting columns rising up three stories. We felt as though we had been transported into Hogwarts. There were lots of tables laid out for registration and presiding over the whole thing was the hash headmistress.* She was wearing a mortarboard, a gown. open at the front, fishnet stockings and a teddy; she was also wielding a cane. I enjoyed the spectacle until Hyacinth told me to stop gawking.

We registered quickly - no queues here (very efficient Hash in the Cotswolds) and got allocated a room up in the Gods - 3 floors up. Fortunately there was a lift. Unfortunately it was just like the one that James Bond had a fight in while tracking down some bad guys in the film *Diamonds are Forever*. It was frightening to use, with metal doors that had to be both pulled across and secured before it would move. It travelled up in an open cage so I tended to get vertigo. However, we were rewarded by the view from our window, which was spectacular, overlooking the ornamental Italian gardens. It also had the advantage of being at the back of the building so we might get some sleep as the noise from the marquee would not reach us. (Hopefully)

We wandered over to the marquee meeting Cooperman, Snowman and Mongrel on the way. The bar was already open so we sampled a half of lager and discussed the beer with Snowman. He was quite encouraged by the Badger and was on his third pint already. The marquee was most impressive, done out with St Trinians memorabilia; several hashers were wearing their 70s fancy dress ready for the evening disco.

Returning to the school we queued for the food. This took ages and when we arrived we got a small chilli con carne served up to us by 1960s type dinner ladies ('more than my job's worth to give you more than half a ladle'). It really was not at all filling and I had to go out of the lunch hall to buy a burger from the barbecue set up outside the marquee.

We went back to our room and investigated the goody bag. It contained a school exercise book with information about Churn Valley committee and details about the weekend's events. Lots of graffiti was found on the back page abusing several hashers - ' Windsock is a tart' was the sort of level being aimed for. There were also fish net stockings for the Saturday St Trinians disco; several condoms, a

---

The theme for the weekend was St Trinians

9: Nash Hash in the Cotswolds

blow up pillow and an excellent quality full-colour T-shirt. Not bad as goody bags go!

We then dressed in our 70s gear - a pair of jeans and a shirt loud enough to be heard over the band for me, a slinky pair of trousers and two tone top for Hyacinth. I also wore an Afro wig and peace symbol although the peace symbol tended to balance on top of my stomach rather than hanging down, and the Afro wig was a little too warm to keep on for long.

The opening ceremony involved a dance routine to *insiwinsy teeny weenie yellow polka dot bikini* with one of the guys running naked across the stage. Mongrel also enjoyed the rendition of *Who let the Dogs Out*. There were lots of tank tops; a fairly gruesome one was worn by Mini Hah Ha. Five Bar was dressed up as a superb Jimmy Saville with a serious cigar. Also a 118 118 man advertising directory enquiries,

P-rick was given a down down for being over-keen to attend. He had registered and paid twice, sending off two application forms and cheques, thus being the only person there with two registration numbers. His excuse was that he had been drunk the first time he filled it in and paid, so did not remember. Must be true - I can't really see P-rick paying twice; it's hard enough to get a beer out of him once!

There was an ostrich with a very realistic head controlled by some cords on the end of its neck. It moved around the dance floor like a psychopathic Rod Hull, attacking anyone who got too close. Now I know how Michael Parkinson must have felt!

Just outside the marquee we got chatting to some American visitors who said that Hashing was really taking off in America. They said that the hash names were much ruder over there. I won't give any examples. However they said that when joining a hash you had to be careful that it was the type you wanted. They have specialised Bike Only Hashes (Bash) that don't do any running at all. Psycho Hashes that only run ball breakers and Naked Hashes that only run without clothes. Standard Isle of Wight type hashes were becoming difficult to find.

The free bar was open all night and considerable amounts of beer were consumed. It always amazes me that there can be so much beer drunk and yet there is never any trouble; hashers really are very decent people.

The only security was one guy dressed in a yellow plastic top with security written across his back.* The police had been informed about the event but were quite happy. The police said that they had never heard of any problems at hash parties and the only reason they wanted to be informed was in case the hash had any outsiders trying to gate crash and drink free beer. Where else can you see people aged between 18 and 80 mixing together, drinking beer and having fun? It really was a super atmosphere.

Breakfast was again a bit of a disappointment: one piece of bacon, one sausage and a bit of scrambled egg, filled out with some toast. We were instructed to collect our packed lunches from the entrance hall then get on the buses for the runs. Poor Sod was still hungry after the meagre food served up for breakfast so he took two lunches and ate one straight away.

I wandered out towards the bus park trying to decide which run to go for. I was amazed to see that the Ball Breaker bus was the first one full, with Cooperman on the front seat! There were lots of hares selling their 'wears' so to speak and eventually I decided on the Three Peaks Run. The hares were Ebley Full Moon and it was an A to B, starting from Coaly picnic site - about 5 miles long. The hares also told me it had lots of short cuts and it was flat! Call me naïve if you like but the hare was so convincing I believed a run with the name Three Peaks would be flat and an A to B run can have short cuts!

We arrived at the start of the run and Mongrel appeared out of the other coach. We started at the top of a hill and ran half a mile down a false trail. We met P-rick coming back the other way as he had gone on the right trail but couldn't find any flour. The trail lived up to its name involving 3 peaks; there were also lots of false trails all of which involved climbing up extra hills. I learnt my lesson after the first false trail. I went jogging happily down into the valley and felt fantastic at being in the front of the pack. I hurled abuse at all the wussies behind me. However when I discovered it was a false trail I

The next night one of the hash somehow acquired the yellow security jacket. He stood at the door completely naked, except for the yellow top, checking the wrist bands of hashers to make sure they had paid! I am just relieved that the police did not arrive to see who was in charge of security

9: Nash Hash in the Cotswolds

realised I would have to climb up the vertical hill in front of me. This enabled me to meet up with a very smug pack of runners who had stayed on the flat.

P-rick sang the hash song *"She's alright she's alright a little flat chested but she's all right"* to what he thought was a passing hasher. In fact she was nothing to do with the hash and was just out jogging! All I can say is, 'It is a good job P-rick can run fast'.

The views were spectacular, looking over the Cotswolds and down to the river Severn Estuary. It was a beautiful sylvan trail along the escarpment, finishing at an Iron Age hill fort. The front-runners kept being caught by line-outs at the bottom of huge downhill sections; they clearly had not learnt from my experience! The hares were not totally honest about the direction the trail was taking! Mongrel always seemed to be just in front of me frolicking along like a puppy; amazing really, considering she went to bed at 3am and slept in one of the showers.

The final peak was small but vicious - it was the sort of mound you see Iron Hill forts built on, surprisingly enough. We short-cutters got to the top and looked at the view, as the rest of the pack came into sight around the corner. They seemed to be heading back to the coach without climbing the hill. This seemed an unreasonable short cut so we all started singing 'More beer, more beer' and they changed direction and came up the hill in search of beer. When they finally struggled up to the top we informed them that all the beer was back in the coach. They didn't find this very funny - no sense of humour some people!

There were a few down downs by the coach: P-rick was given one for going the wrong way: I was given one for saying I couldn't drink because I was taking Hyacinth shopping that afternoon. The reaction was, 'You are at Nash hash. You should be drinking, not shopping!' Mongrel was given one for not booking accommodation and converting a shower to a bedroom.

On returning, I had a conversation in the showers with some local hashers. 'Take a Look' said she went on the Cider with Rosie run. It was very pretty but there were three grumpy old blokes from the Isle of Wight on the run with them. I couldn't work out who these three were as no one from the Isle of Wight had said they were going on the Cider with Rosie run.

The afternoon was spent shopping; we needed to get our St Trinians outfits together for the evening disco. Hyacynth and I went into the town of Tetbury, a small market town about 2 miles down the road. It was a super spot with typical Cotswold stone buildings, antique shops and a profusion of pubs. Apparently the town dates back to a prehistoric hill fort. In AD681 a monastery was built on the site that was supervised by the Abbess Tetta hence the name of the town.

The town has a long association with the wool trade and there is an annual sack race. This race involves lots of mad people running up a 1:4 hill with a 60 lb sack of wool on their back, usually after drinking large quantities of ale. (I am sure hashers would feel very much at home competing!)

We chose the Crown Inn for lunch, a quiet country type pub with a large and varied menu. We waited for ages to get served; this was because there was only one girl on the bar serving drinks, taking food orders and delivering food to the tables. She was terrific, doing her best to give everyone good service while rushing from pillar to post. The food itself was mediocre. Hyacinth suggested that the roast dinner came from a cow that must have lived several years in a retirement home before it was slaughtered. Even so, I gave the waitress a good tip as I really appreciated how hard she worked to keep everyone happy in very trying circumstances.

We then walked along the high street and found a second hand clothes shop. Some of the clothes in these shops are amazing - Jaeger designer wear - almost immaculate dresses for £5; a bargain I thought. Unfortunately there was no way I would fit in a size 10. I eventually found a tent cum skirt in black and a white shirt that looked vaguely like school uniform. Combined with fish net stockings a wig and a school tie I looked just like a St Trinians school girl. I came out of the dressing room to show Hyacinth the full effect.

There was another couple in the shop at the time and they gave me a really strange look. He then said, 'I don't know how you can dress up like that, it is an abomination.' Rather than telling him to mind his own business I explained that it was for a party up at Westonbirts School and the theme was St Trinnians. He was shocked at the idea that there could be hundreds of us all dressed up as schoolgirls. I don't think he was the type to recruit into the hash! If he had found out some of the things that go on at hash events he would have joined a monastery there and then.

9: Nash Hash in the Cotswolds

We returned to the school and went for a tour around the ornamental gardens. They were a dazzling array of terraced plants, Italianate walled gardens and water features. In the arboretum there are six trees designated by the tree register as championship trees. This means they are the largest or tallest trees of their kind in the world. The 400-acre site is actually described in the Doomsday Book. It seemed a bizarre contrast - the tourists happily taking photographs of the gardens, accompanied by the sounds of drunken hashers singing a very inappropriate song about a dicky dido.

I chatted to P-rick about the Shiggy run. He said that they had met up with the bike hash (bash) on route and there had ensued a huge water fight by the lake. Mad Dog lived up to his name by going bonkers when he had a bucket of water poured over him. He chased after the culprit like a man possessed.

Meanwhile Fat Bastard had picked up Mad Dog's bike and proceeded to ride it into the lake. He kept his balance all the way to the middle then turned the bike upside down burying it in the mud. On his return, Mad Dog turned into Bloody Furious Dog as he had to get his bike out of several feet of mud in the middle of the lake. The Shiggy runners were by this time so covered in mud that no one could be recognised, Big Dump even had a toadstool growing on his head.

The rest of the afternoon was spent relaxing, just sitting outside the marquee and chatting to hashers. We got talking to a New Zealander who, it turned out, lived on the same road that Hyacinth used to live on when she was in Auckland - it is a small world!

Eventually the queue for dinner went down and we headed inside. On his way out was PX who was wearing an apron with a naked Greek god on the front. The back was completely open and he wore nothing underneath. I dread to think what the ladies serving the meagre dinner thought.

The evening's entertainment started at 7 30 with some hash acts - they were not very good, so we sat in Hooker's caravan. We were most entertained by Poor Sod who had lost his voice and sounded like something from the Godfather. This malady started in Eurohash and was rapidly spreading through all present. It was rumoured to be passed on by snogging and Twonk was thought to be an asymptomatic carrier. Poor Sod really should be more picky about who he snogs. Snowman informed us that Fracas, Hooker and himself had not been able to get on the Avebury run so had to go on the Cider with Rosie run instead!

As the hash acts finished and the band began we wandered over to the marquee and danced to classics like The Moody Blues, Blondie, Blues Brothers and, of course, at a St Trinians disco, School's Out by Alice Cooper.

The outfits were excellent, everyone looked like St Trinians school-girls, both the men and women. Those hashers serving behind the bar decided to take off most of their clothes. I did tell one of the girls who served me some beer that I felt her school uniform was a disgrace; she was only wearing a Bra and panties! She stuck her tongue out and removed her bra. 'Is that better?' she asked.

A bubble machine was set up in the corner of the marquee and a wall of bubbles slowly progressed across the dance floor. Then something went wrong and the bubbles stopped. There was the most dreadful smell from the machine. I do not know what substance was leaking out but I can only describe the smell as an acrid chemical silage aroma. It cleared half of the dance floor in about 2 minutes; no one would return until the device was switched off. I was glad we did not dive into the bubbles as some of those that did had to wash their clothes three times to get rid of the smell.

Hyacinth and I headed for bed at about 1 am. On the way back I caught one of the hashers smoking behind the marquee - disgraceful behaviour. I told her she should not be smoking in uniform - it was against school rules. She bent over and said 'Yes I am very naughty you had better spank me.' It was a good job that Hyacinth did not notice this as she is a social worker and I would have been in trouble from the Children's Act!

Monday was the hangover run. This was an enormous affair - 300 hashers running through the arboretum. I have never been in such a large pack. It was also a very long run for a hangover event and I felt like getting a taxi by the end. I met Carol on the trail. She used to hash with the Isle of Wight but now lives in Saudi Arabia. She had arrived at the event on Friday then spent 16 hours behind the bar. Seems a strange thing to do, but I suppose if you have been in Saudi for 6 months and not allowed to touch alcohol, working behind a free bar has its attractions.

Chapter 10

The Isle of Wight Thousandth Run

The venue, as usual, for this major IOW hash event was Ventnor Rugby club. I always find navigating on the Isle of Wight easier if I imagine it as a clock face. Cowes is at 12 o'clock and Blackgang at 6 o'clock with Ryde at 2 o'clock. Ventnor is at 4 o'clock. The Rugby club is on the main road that runs between Ventnor and Blackgang. The view from the pitch is spectacular as it is at the top of an almost vertical incline that leads down to the sea. There is a public footpath opposite the club that leads down to Steep Hill Cove, which is very aptly named.

The other three sides have hills, so the club is in a sort of natural amphitheatre with the sea being where the actors would perform. It really is very beautiful and, when not full of noisy hashers, tranquil and relaxing. I doubt there are many Rugby clubs in the country that have a better setting.

Ventnor is on the south east coast of the Isle of Wight 'at 4 o'clock'. It is predicted that global warming will cause it to slide into the sea within 100 years - if you want to see it, go soon! Other parts of the island have similar problems - if you want to see some parts of Blackgang you need to go there within the next few minutes!

Tanglefoot and Godot live in a house in Niton '7 o'clock' that is currently falling into the sea. This is incredibly brave; they used to have a huge garden and glass summerhouse - now both the summerhouse and the garden reside on Niton beach. The section of the house they currently live in has a huge crack down the middle and the place creaks as one section of land slides past the other. It is like a miniature version of the San Andreas Fault line. How they sleep at night with a huge drop beckoning over the cliff is beyond me.

I arrived in Ventnor on the Friday night with Fracas and we got down to setting up our tents. There was a fair old breeze coming off the hills so it was quite a battle to stop the tents blowing away. We were in a hurry as the run/pub-crawl was due to start at 6.30 and we only just finished in time. There were about 130 people booked in for the weekend and it was great to see so many familiar faces. Mini Ha ha, Twonk, Netto, Commercial Whale, Fat Bastard, Magnum and Twilight to name just a few.

IOW hash weekends are incredibly popular and the event was sold out six months before. I must say that those on the committee who organise the event do a superb job - the beer is always good and the food excellent. The hares have masses of beautiful countryside to set the runs in and they make the most of it (80% of the Isle of Wight is designated as an area of outstanding natural beauty).

It was called the Red Run as it was the May Day Bank Holiday weekend and many of us were wearing our red dresses; my old maternity outfit from Arhus was resurrected. I must say some of the girls looked stunning in ball gowns they had purchased from e bay for five pounds. Rainmaker and Boycee looked ready to go to the hunt ball. It really was a shame to destroy them by running through mud, then again it is hashing, so running is what it is all about. We headed up into the hills behind the Rugby club and jogged along rough paths as best we could in our red dresses.

After about a mile we came out on to the road and headed for the social club and a beer stop. The Religious Advisor Mr Magoo presided over some down downs. Commercial Whale got one for the best blow job! His blow up mattress had exploded; he had done the usual trick of connecting it to the electric air pump on his car and then went off in search of beer.
I got one for finding my way to the hash, very out of character for Navigator! We had a quick beer and then headed down the road, past

10: The Isle of Wight Thousandth Run

the dip in the ground where Ventnor railway station used to stand. It is such a shame that the line was closed in the 60s - it looks a fabulous place in old photographs that adorn the walls of many local pubs.

We kept running downhill in the direction of the Crab and Lobster Tap. I was chatting to Thong from some northern hash on the way down. She said, 'The last time I saw you was at Nash Hash when you were painting my breasts pink. I said, 'I don't think I was; I am sure it is the sort of thing I would remember!' However if she fancied an action replay I would be willing to paint them in the hope that it would come back to me. Sadly she declined my offer.

The Crab and Lobster is a terrific pub with thousands of knick-knacks placed on every available surface. There are historic adverts on the walls explaining why in the 1930s you should have eaten Marmite and drunk Guinness. The food is very reasonably priced and you can have a bottle of pleasant wine with your meal for about six pounds.

The only thing I don't like is that the landlord is a rabid anti European and he has lots of propaganda stating why we should come out of the European Community. I have heard that 80% of our jobs depend on us trading with Europe so I feel he is a little misguided. Whenever I eat there I always leave a tip in Euros!

Some more down downs went on but it was too noisy to hear what was being said, so a few of us headed onto pub number three, the Volunteer. This is the smallest pub on the Isle of Wight consisting of a front room with seating for about 20 and a back room with seating for 15. A tiny bar circles round into both rooms. It is a very friendly place and the beer is well kept. However, I did feel it was not quite the ideal pub to bring 100 hashers into.

Those of us in the advance party got a beer in quickly and we grabbed the few available seats. As the hash turned up it felt like a record attempt trying to get as many people as possible into the smallest pub on the island. It was impossible to stand up and difficult to breathe - the locals who were sitting having a quiet pint did not know what had hit the place. We rapidly escaped to pub number four The Blenheim.

The Blenheim is large enough to accommodate 100 people. On Friday nights it has a superb Karaoke. When we got in no one was singing. I went straight up and requested Summer Nights from

Grease; I was accompanied by several Harriets. I did the John Travolta bit and they did the Olivia Newton John part. P-rick arrived and went straight into a Beatles number, then everyone just sang together to American Pie, Bohemian Rhapsody and numerous other songs. Everyone was having so much fun that we all decided to stay in this pub and not follow the map on to pub number 5.

Snowman remarked that 'Karaoke only works when people are in the mood for it' (or possibly when they are pissed enough!). We have tried having Karaoke sessions after the hash dinner and no one would join in, but every time we turn up at The Blenhiem pub on a Friday night we can't get the hash off the microphone. The singing went on past last orders and eventually the Karaoke DJ (if that is the right term?) turned off the power.

We were in the centre of Ventnor and the Rugby club was up a vertical incline 2 miles away. There was no chance of a taxi at this time of night as all the pubs had just rung last orders and Ventnor is only a one-horse town. We were just getting ready for the horrendous climb when around the corner came Trevor (Bart) in the minibus. 'I love you Trevor, and I want to have your babies!' I said to him as we piled on! Twilight could not believe the superb organisation of The Isle of Wight hash. Just as we come out of the pub a free minibus appears! Fantastic!

We arrived back at the Rugby club and Trevor, star that he is, went back into town for another load. There were burgers cooking for those with the munchies and the beer was flowing freely in every sense of the word. It was a great atmosphere although I was shattered by this time and retired to my tent. It was freezing cold and difficult to get to sleep with all the noise from the clubhouse - even ear-plugs would not block out the low frequencies. I eventually drifted off at about 2am. I was rudely awoken by Fracas playing the Last Post on his bugle at 6.30 am IN THE MORNING!!! I threatened to bury him under a bloody post if he made any more noise.

After that I had to give up on sleep. I tried to drift off again and some antisocial bastard played the stereo in their car at full blast. I decided to go for an early shower before they got full up. Then I went for breakfast. This was excellent. There was plenty of it, a full English with bacon, eggs, sausage, fried bread, tomatoes, fresh orange juice, tea and coffee. This was really super food, an ideal energy source for running; slow release carbohydrates are also a wonderful cure for hangovers.

10: The Isle of Wight Thousandth Run

The coaches arrived about 11am and we all got on for the runs. Interloper appeared with Stalker but there was no room on the coach so once again Trevor and his mini bus came to the rescue. The runs were over in Calbourne, home of the only working water mill on the Isle of Wight. This is virtually the other end of the island from Ventnor (8 o'clock). However, it gave the Hashers from England the chance to see the scenery. We passed out of Ventnor and one of the visitors felt the scenery was like travelling through Wales, hills rising on one side and steep drops to the sea below on the other. But the scenery changed rapidly and other Hashers thought it looked more like the Yorkshire dales as we passed Niton.

A little further on and we came to the Military Road. This runs along the length of the south coast of the island; driving along it always reminds me of Cornwall. I have always felt that the Isle of Wight has a miniature version of every type of scenery found in Britain. It is an astonishing place, particularly the bits that are not falling into the sea!

As we drove down the Military Road several hashers from the mainland thought we must have been going around in circles, as the island couldn't possibly be so large. I was sitting next to Flip Top who asked me where we were. I warned him that he was talking to Navigator and my directions should not be relied on.

We eventually arrived at the site for the runs. We then waited 10 minutes for the other bus to catch up (It arrived after us, yet started off before us. Bizarre!). I considered going on the long run; Interloper and Boycee tried to persuade me that it wouldn't be much further than the other run. However, I took one look at those on the run, a fit looking bunch, and headed for the short trail.

Tanglefoot and Godot laid the short trail in their usual inimitable style. The first section was over Brighstone Down then over towards Hulverstone. The views would have been spectacular except there was a thick mist that obscured anything beyond about half a mile. We climbed; we climbed and then climbed some more. I was beginning to think this was the first hash in history that was set all uphill.

Then suddenly we began the descent. This was seriously steep and it was difficult to see where we were going because of the mist. It actually became fairly dangerous to run and even walking had to be done with care.

We passed on to the Long Stone, the remains of a Neolithic long barrow (dated at 2500 years BC). It consists of three large stones arranged so the one at the front is formed like an altar. It is said that they used to sacrifice virgins to the Gods at this very spot. However, the practice does not go on today, as there is no chance of finding a virgin on the Isle of Wight. Gods are in short supply too!

We ran over Brighstone Down and on the other side we could see the keen hashers climbing up yet another hill. Several took the shortcut down to the road but I decided to continue and trotted along beside Floss.

She was in reflective mood and said how wonderful the hash was, how she treated them as an extended family and what a great bunch of people they were to be with. If you have got a problem you can guarantee one of the hash will be willing and able to help you out. I personally couldn't agree more; we sometimes forget what a great institution the Hash is.

We came back to the road and headed into the Sun Inn at Hulverstone; a classic country pub with a superb beer garden. By now the mist had cleared and the sun was shining down on the world. It was superb: a glorious spring day; a country pub garden and entertaining company. What more could anyone ask out of life?

After an hour or so we continued along the trail running, down the road and then turning right into some serious shiggy. There was mud everywhere and if you slipped there were plenty of stinging nettles to get your legs. Rainmaker was covered in mud by Mark E Mark who then got some cow manure thrown on his bald patch. 'Now that's what I call a pat on the head!' he said and ran on, smelling of cow.

Eventually we arrived at Mottistone Manor, this is an Elizabethan Manor House situated at the foot of the downs 2 miles west of Brighstone. There is a terraced garden in a wooded valley, with an herbaceous border and some super views of the English Channel. The Mottistone estate extends 263 hectares from Mottistone down to the coast at Sudmoor.

Collecting our packed lunches from the waiting coaches (superb organisation by the IOW Hash Committee again) we retired to the green to wait for the long runners to appear. They eventually turned up after seven long miles looking remarkably clean; they had clearly

10: The Isle of Wight Thousandth Run

avoided the shiggy that the short runners went through. We were all back on the coaches and returned to Ventnor in what felt like no time.

The evening event was sixties theme flour power (Yes it is a joke not bad spelling on my part) I managed to wear a very brightly coloured shirt and the blue wig from Eurohash. I said proudly to a passing hasher that this shirt makes a statement! 'Yes, it says Prat!' he replied. Hyacynth turned up wearing a psychedelic coloured top, a red headband and a peace symbol.

The mantra of love and peace was chanted by us as we walked to the dance floor - Love and peace, Love and peace, Love on Peace off! The entertainment started with the Yorkshire Hash (Wheels and Co) playing some superb guitar in a sing along. We had *Mrs Robinson* from The Graduate, *Living Doll* by Cliff Richard and *American Pie*, to name but a few. Everyone joined in the singing; it was all terrific fun and the atmosphere was electric - although the Guitars were acoustic!

The disco started up and played some classics from the 60s 70s and 80s; the DJ said should we leave the nineties alone and everyone cheered. So we had a great night of disco music without any dark heavy base or techno row. Brilliant! The flour power theme was universal with everyone joining in the spirit of the evening.

I went for an early night being shagged out by all the bugle playing from Fracas in the morning. I managed to miss the hangover run, sleep being more important, but caught the end of the down downs.

Boycee got one for not wearing hash gear on runs. She was given a free hash T shirt to wear. However, she said she had some hash tops but did not like to wear them. She wanted to be taken for a serious runner not a piss head. Never has a down down been more richly deserved.

LC got one for being noisy. She was in high spirits all the way through the flour power party: dancing on tables; singing at the top of her voice and shouting raucously. She was asked by one of the visitors what LC stood for, 'Lara Croft' she told them, 'as the hash think I look just like her.' 'Are you sure it doesn't stand for loud cow?' he asked, and received a very long stare.

There was a bra that was lost en route the previous night. It was reunited with its delectable owner. Sadly she did not drink the beer out of the cups, claiming they were too small to hold a pint.

The afternoon was glorious as we all sat in the sun catching some rays and finishing off the beer. The Yorkshire guitarists tuned up again and Magnum joined them kicking a tin bath in rhythm to the music as a sort of impromptu floorshow. It was really very pleasant, (the atmosphere, not Magnum's floor show) good beer, sunny weather, a sing song and a view across the Channel for miles and miles.

Apparently, Poor Sod took lots of the visitors sailing on Monday. This must have been interesting as there was at least a force 7 blowing across the Solent and it was torrential rain. He is not called Poor Sod for nothing!

Chapter 11

And Then There Was Essex

Essex had their 1001st run on the weekend of Friday the 28th of May. Fracas and I decided to go on this event, as it was only a short drive up the country. The theme was 1001 Arabian nights the; flyer had a magic carpet on it being flown by a mystical looking Arab.

We got the ferry across to Portsmouth on Friday afternoon and drove along the south coast towards Worthing then headed North along the A24 up to the M25. This is a lot faster than going North through Guildford on a bank holiday weekend, I can highly recommend it. We made great time up to the Dartford crossing; however the queue for the tunnel was horrendous.

I read once that the Dartford tunnel was built using taxpayers money and that it would only charge for people to use it until the cost of building it was repaid. I didn't notice any signs stating it is now free; perhaps that nice Mrs Thatcher sold it off in the 80s!

We turned off towards Grays and Thurock, passing the huge Lakeside shopping centre on the way. It was like driving into the Bronx; the whole place felt tatty and depressing and there was graffiti everywhere. The high-rise blocks were poorly maintained and they had obviously just had an appeal for litter, as it was everywhere you looked.

We drove into Thurrock Rugby club and things looked a little better. The actual club was fairly pleasant. However, as soon as we got out of the car we were told to lock it. 'Don't even think about dropping your stuff at the end of the field without locking the car or it will be gone!' warned a passing hasher who seemed to take pleasure in telling everyone how dreadful the area was.

The club was a large rectangular building with a grandstand at the front overlooking three Rugby pitches, one of which was floodlit. All the windows had heavy shutters ready to padlock up. At the end of the pitches the land continued as fields into the distance. The view was only slightly marred by several dual carriageways, enough electricity pylons to power NASA, and a mobile phone mast.

We put up our tents (after locking and alarming the car twice) at the end of the floodlit pitch. We could clearly hear the hum of the overhead pylons. 'Why do electricity pylons hum?', asked a passing hasher. 'Because they don't know the words came the reply!'

The Friday night run was set by Windsock and was predictably a walk, well a pub-crawl. We headed across one of the dual carriageways into what could loosely be called countryside. Our first pub on route was tiny. About eighty of us attempted to get into the snug bar. It may have been possible except there were two Essex men in there with the largest stomachs I have ever seen. They really were barrels; the rest of their body was not particularly large, the stomach just came out and defied gravity.

Fracas and I got beer and retired to the garden where several very drunk Harriets' tried to talk to us. They had serious Essex accents and we really could not understand what they were on about. One of the more military type hashers commented in posh tones 'Oh I knew I had forgotten to pack something, my Essex to English dictionary!'

We walked on to the next pub. It is difficult to describe the area; it is semi rural with horrible blocks of flats scattered around the place. The shops we came to had boarded up windows. Most of the houses we passed had two or three cars parked in the drive or on the lawn.

11: And Then There Was Essex

Some houses looked neat - middle class dwellings with well-kept lawns and double garages. Others were done out in Dell Boy style, bizarre colour schemes and tacky wishing wells. Next door to these would be houses with gardens that looked like scrap yards: a burnt out white van sitting on the lawn; rubbish everywhere and a pile of old bricks in the corner.

We were one of the first to arrive at the next pub, which was frighteningly run down and looked as though the outside covered area was about to collapse. Even the huge garden benches were chained up; how anyone could pick one up to steal it I don't know.

Inside, one of the hares was getting the third degree from an irate Essex man. He seemed to think he owned the bar and told him that this was Sharon's birthday party and he didn't want people in here. The barmaid disagreed and said it was still open to the public. He was starting to get aggressive when another ten hashers appeared.

How many more are coming he asked 'another ten?' 'Oh more than that' replied the hare. 'Well how many then?' said Essex man 'about a hundred replied the hare.' Essex man sat down and went quiet; he must have thought that even Sharon and all her brothers could not intimidate a hundred people - although Sharon was pretty frightening!

We all piled in and headed for the karaoke. Wild Thing rang out, followed by the Rolling Stones. I did Summer Nights with Mongrel. Unfortunately she didn't know how a karaoke worked and she ended up singing all the wrong lines.

The notice on the wall said 'Sharon's party all welcome.' However there were only five of them there all night. They were clearly very bored, Sharon started warming to the hash and even the Essex man decided to sing along to the karaoke.

Arriving back at the Rugby club the disco had started, which was pretty good. However, there was no free beer, we had to pay £2.40 for a pint of lager behind the bar.

In the corner there were about 20 barrels of beer set up as a 'mini beer festival' Fracas tried a couple of them (at a pound a half), said they were disgusting and went on to lager (for him this is sacrilege - the beer must have been diabolical).

However in fairness they were serving free burgers from the barbeque outside. Windsock and Tops came around with some wicked cocktails at midnight so we did get something for our money on Friday night.

We all had a bit of a boogie (it was a good disco) and I went off to bed about 12.30 am. I attempted to get to sleep but the couple in the tent three places away were having what I can only describe as record-breaking sex; it was certainly capable of breaking eardrums! Even with ear-plugs firmly rammed in I could still hear, 'Stand up, bend over, no the other way, that's it yes, yes, do it harder big boy!' In the morning a whole crowd of hashers stood outside their tent and gave them a round of applause as they got up!

The next day was slightly overcast and humid. I missed breakfast and went into the superb showers, plenty of them, and very hot.

On the way back I met Mongrel who was outside her tent with some ant killer. Apparently she was infested with ants and had surrounded her tent with a circle of white powder. This seemed like a good idea. However, as she didn't know how many ants were already inside the circle of powder, she was just as likely to trap them in as keep them out. As it was the whole nest turned out to be under her tent so she later got a down down for stupidity!

We met for the start of the run at 11am. I chose the long run, which, we were told, was only an hour and a half. We went across one of the areas of common land next to the Rugby club. The pack was running so fast I saw red shift in the sunlight. We slowed down to sub-light speed as we approached the dual carriageway. Across the road we went down our first public footpath. It was a disgrace: there was rubbish and broken bottles everywhere; overgrown with weeds and used as a toilet at regular intervals, not just by dogs either, there was used toilet roll scattered about the place. We ran on across roads, through shabby towns and up the only hill in Essex.

We got a view of the Thames and could see a cruise liner moored at the side of the river. I hope it was being repaired, as I cannot imagine Grays being a tourist destination for those on a cruise. Yes, you have seen the acropolis, the pyramids, been into Rhodes harbour, next you are going to see a complete shit hole up the Thames estuary!

11: And Then There Was Essex

There was a small village, with a green and a pub, where a couple of us got a coke. However, this was an hour and a quarter into the run and there was no sign of heading back. I decided on a short cut but Fracas continued on the trail. We went down some more horrible paths and passed a farm that seemed to grow tyres, there were fields full of them. Even among the crops of wheat and barley growing in most of the other fields, there was always a shrubbery of tyres.

After 2 hours of the worst run I have ever been on we arrived a few yards up the road from the Karaoke pub. There was a barrel set up on the common near the high-rise flats (where Sharon and her brothers lived) and we could get some free beer.

Mongrel decided she did not want beer and got a lift from someone to get a bottle of wine. She came back with an expensive Cava and was given grief for being on the dole and buying £20 bottles of wine!

After another hour the non-short cutters arrived, making it three hours, yes three hours, running through essentially a rubbish tip. Fracas looked like death and collapsed on the ground; he had to be revived with several pints of beer.

It was then back to the clubhouse and a Cornish pasty lunch. The clubhouse was now full of people watching a Rugby match on a huge screen; there was no atmosphere of being on a hash and no free beer.

The afternoon was really boring until dinner was served at 6pm. It was okay, a reasonable curry and lasagne - still no free beer. Fracas and I had had enough by now; the Rugby was still blasting in the background; you couldn't talk. 'Let's go and find a nice pub I suggested.' 'Yeh we can have a look around Grays and see what is about', said Fracas.'

We walked across the common outside the club and were pursued by various kids on motorbikes who seemed to think it was amusing to ride as close to pedestrians as possible, without actually hitting them. There was a white building on the right, which was apparently a leisure centre, but it was impossible to read the sign because of the graffiti all over it.
We took our life into our hands as we crossed the road near a roundabout, motorists in Essex did not seem to know what indicators were. We headed for the only pub visible in the centre of Grays The

'Kings Urine' I think it was called. The outside was in a poor state of repair; the windows rotten, and the brickwork crumbling.

Inside it was worse than the Rugby club. This time football was blasting out of every orifice. Everyone was dressed casually but in very sombre colours. We were wearing the Isle of Wight flour power shorts and very bright T-shirts - we should have just written 'Not Local'on our foreheads.

We struggled through the crowds to the bar and ordered a couple of beers. Fracas was accosted by a local who said 'You from the Isle of Wight then.' 'Yes' Fracas replied, "Can you get us cheap tickets for the Isle of Wight festival then?" 'No' said Fracas 'we are not going.' "Yeh but you could get us tickets can't you" 'No' said Fracas. "Why not" said Essex man getting aggressive. 'Because they are sold out,' said Fracas. This seemed to mollify him a bit although he still didn't look happy.

'Oh look' I said 'there is a beer garden. Shall we go out?' We escaped Essex man by walking towards the back door. The beer garden was a car park, with a few benches on the side. The first bench had a large crowd of skinheads who looked like they were dealing drugs. We had to squeeze past their table to get through the door. Sitting as far away as possible we drank our beers as fast as possible and endured continual stares from the bald drug barons!

There were no other pubs in the area so we decided the Rugby club wasn't as bad as we thought and returned. The band was in full flow and the disco again was good. Still no free beer. However, Windsock and Topps came to the rescue again with some free cocktails. For some reason the party just didn't get going. I think everyone was knackered from the nine mile run.

We enjoyed the cocktails and drank on until midnight. The naked run was announced and a number of hashers went outside and took off their clothes. They went for a short run around a floodlit rugby pitch. The local members of the rugby club were absolutely astonished
The next day we packed away our tents and headed home. We were not at all disappointed to be leaving Essex.

Chapter 12

Interhash 2004 Cardiff

The M4 goes across the River Severn estuary on a spectacular suspension bridge. It is just awesome; the river looks tiny underneath it. However it is also a work of art. The steel supports laid symmetrically in elegant patterns, form interlacing triangles. Beautiful to look at, and high enough up to give you vertigo, it is a modern equivalent of the Clifton suspension bridge, built by Isombard Kingdom Brunell a few miles back, up a branch of the same river.

Once across you have entered Wales; country of hills, valleys, male voice choirs and sheep fanciers. The approach to the city of Cardiff (Europe's youngest capital - we were regularly told by passing signs), is made through a short tunnel passing under an inconvenient hill (Wales has a large number of these). The main road then becomes a dual carriageway with lots of signs saying 'Permanent speed camera just ahead, slow down now.' It is very decent of the Welsh to give specific information about the location of these 20th century highwaymen. Everyone slows down as they approach the danger spot and they achieve what they are intended to do without filling the Chancellor's coffers.

In England they are usually hidden behind a bush and the speed limit signs just disappear as you approach them. Time and again I have done 30 miles an hour on a dual carriageway because I have seen lots of signs for speed cameras but no indication of what the speed limit actually is. If anyone can tell me what the speed limit is on the A446 between Sutton Coldfield and the Belfrey golf centre I will give them a prize! Why can they not put a speed limit sign under the camera warning?

The route to the city centre is well sign posted in both Welsh and English. We follow the signs towards the city hall where we hope to register for the Interhash weekend. The city is busy on this drizzly Thursday afternoon and our progress through the city centre is not helped by the three thousand hashers wearing red dresses who are running everywhere and calling 'On you'.

The expressions on the faces of other drivers can only be described as astonishment. A rather overweight hairy male hasher has just crossed over in front of us; he looks like a pink mountain dressed in one of Evans over size shops maternity outfits. The girls behind him look really elegant, if a little bizarre, wearing red evening gowns and running shoes. The red dress runners have paid £15 each to join in and all this money goes to a children's charity.

We eventually manage to park in a multi-storey car park behind the Walkabout pub; this is where all the red dress runners are heading for the Down Downs. We walk against the tide of red, heading for city hall and registration. After about half a mile Hyacinth and I are lost. We ask some passing red-clad figures the way to registration only to be told that it has already closed. Now we do not know what to do; we have no idea where the halls of residence are that we are staying in and we do not even know if we will be able to get a key when we do find them.

Snowman had arranged the accommodation and by racking my brains I remembered that he said the accommodation was at a place called Column Hall. A nearby map revealed the location of the halls only a mile away. We drove over there and found a reception area open and issuing keys. The hash may seem like a bunch of disorganised drunkards but they actually have the organisational skills of top managers. In fact it is not really that surprising. Lots of hashers are top professionals. However, they never talk about what they do,

12: Interhash 2004 Cardiff

only who they run with. This is very refreshing at least in Britain where what you do seems almost as important as your right arm.

The halls were great; students today do not know they are born. The rooms have en-suite facilities, connection for computers to the Internet; windows that actually open more than 20 centimetres; and beds suitable for lots of student shagging.

We dumped our bags and headed into town. At the front of the shopping centre is a statue of Aneurin Bevan the founder of the National Health Service. His creation was one of the greatest, most wonderful things that anyone could do. Health treatment free at the point of need, where would we be without it? His ideas spread across the world and civilised countries everywhere now have free health care.

We still have a health service, despite the Conservatives' efforts to starve it of funds and privatise it in the 1980s. I cannot imagine living in a country where children are sent home from hospital to die just because their parents cannot afford the medical bills. What a terrific achievement it was managing to get the National Health Service Act through parliament when the country was almost bankrupt after the Second World War.

We walked down from the town centre to the Walkabout pub where the hash was meeting. This was so packed that it was impossible to get in. It was around 7pm and we decided to find a curry house. This proved very difficult. We looked around the shopping centre and down all the side streets. Cardiff City Centre just did not seem to have any Indian restaurants at all. In the end we had to make do with a Chinese. We went to the Noble House Chinese restaurant on Wood Street which was not bad at all but a little expensive.

Snowman phoned through on his mobile asking if we knew where a curry house was as they all wanted to eat. We told him the bad news, Cardiff being the Marie Celeste of curry house world.

We wandered out of the Chinese and headed back to hash central; the Walkabout pub and Sam's bar just across the road. Both of these places were absolutely packed with red clad hashers. Sam's garden was a sea of red, so we headed across for a beer. Hyacinth managed to commandeer the end of a bench so I went inside to get some drinks. As I went in a wall of sound from the disco hit me. Mongrel was gyrating along with Magnum and Twilight to Blame it on the Boogy by Michael Jackson. I ran over, gave her a hug and grabbed some drinks from the bar.

I headed back outside with beer and a dry Martini. Hyacinth was chatting to Les Oeff from Denmark: he was advertising the Danish hash jubilee weekend. There are now so many events going on that it must be possible to go to a large hash event every weekend. Provided you remember to pack your spare liver you should be fine!

We went into the disco and had a fun hour dancing to some great sounds of the seventies and the eighties. It is difficult to describe how friendly hash events are. Everyone is there to have a good time and we all have hashing in common, so you end up talking to total strangers as though they are old friends.

I went down to the loo in the basement and regretted it immediately. I will not describe the scene but as someone had had it coming out of both ends, an oxygen mask would have been useful. I came back up stairs and went next door to the Casablanca Italian restaurant they had some lovely loos upstairs.

Hyacynth wondered where I had been so I explained about the toilet situation. She decided she would go next door as well so I went outside and sat on a bench to wait for her. Well I waited and waited and waited. I really wanted to go in and find out what had happened to her. However she was using the toilet in a restaurant where we hadn't eaten or even had a drink so I didn't know what I would say to them.

Eventually she reappeared looking a little white. What happened I asked? Well she said I got to the toilets OK, went in and locked the door. I then tried to get out and the handle fell off the door onto the floor. I tried to pick it up and reinsert it but the lights then went out and I was in complete darkness.

All I could do was bang on the door and call for help. Eventually someone heard me and got two of the waiters from downstairs. I told them what had happened and how it was pitch black inside. They shouted through the door that it was on a movement sensor and that I had to move around to keep the light on. Being only 4 foot 11 inches I was clearly not tall enough for the sensor to detect me so I had to start leaping up into the air. I was locked in the ladies' loo with two

12: Interhash 2004 Cardiff

Italian waiters outside and a queue of desperate female customers all telling me to jump up higher.

I said it was no good I couldn't get the light to work. They said 'Stand back, we will have to shoulder barge the door.' I ran back and tried one last leap - miraculously the light came back on. I told them to hold the shoulder barge and managed to insert the handle in the door again. Fortunately they were far too busy apologising to me about the door lock to ask any questions about why I was in there in the first place.

We had a final beer and decided to head back to the halls of residence. It was quite a long walk and all uphill. When we got into the halls we found our rooms in total darkness. Everywhere else was brightly lit but no lights or plug sockets would work for us. The notice on the wall informed us of where to go for maintenance and even at 12.30 am there was someone on duty to come and reset our trip switch.

The next morning was bright and blustery as we headed for registration at Cardiff city hall. This is a magnificent edifice constructed of white Portland stone in the wedding cake architectural style. There is a clock on top of it that glistens gold in the sunlight. It is apparently not just gold paint but thick gold leaf that covers the fingers and numbers. The bell that chimes in the hours has exactly the same sound as Big Ben in London so when I closed my eyes and listened to it I was transported to Westminster.

Inside it is all marble and white stone with statues everywhere. At the top of the stairs is a statue of Boddecea a heroine from a Welsh tribe who went on to lead the Icini people in a revolt against Roman occupation. Boddecea eventually poisoned herself because she could not face capture.

The place was heaving with hashers, all queuing in a disorderly manner; a riot of colours trying to get registered or to buy lots of hashing memorabilia from the hash haberdashery. The goody bag was excellent. A sturdy haversack with Cardiff Interhash written on the outside, it contained a white raincoat with a cartoon montage on the back of events likely to happen on a hash weekend (beer, running, singing and more beer). Unfortunately from the front it looked like the sort of coat worn by forensic experts at a scene of crime investigation. There was also a wrist bag to carry money about when running.

We went into the hash habberdash and I bought a pair of running shorts with a plastic bum incorporated: they made up in cheapness what they lacked in taste. I thought they would be useful for a party I had been invited to where the theme was to go as a London underground station, 'Arsenal' I thought.

There was not much going on during the afternoon so we decided to explore Cardiff. We headed down to Cardiff bay, the old port area, passing the lights at the entrance that had been donated to Cardiff by Spain after the Barcelona Olympics. We passed the notorious Tiger Bay area where Shirley Bassey used to live and Charlotte Church's boyfriend still does.

The seafront had been yuppified like many of these old industrial areas that are near water. There were lots of shops and restaurants, regular boat trips went across the bay and behind it all was a huge building site where the Wales Millennium Centre for the Performing Arts was being constructed on one side. On the other side was the Welsh National Assembly building. This was a huge white edifice with a curved copper roof that blazed in the midday sun. All the materials for the construction of the Millennium Centre were being sourced in Wales; the only exception was the cloth for the chairs, which came from the Isle of Bute in Scotland.

The visitor centre was unusual in that it looked like the submarine from the 60s television series Voyage to the Bottom of the Sea (The Seaview). I expected to see Admiral Nelson peering out of the porthole and a huge octopus sitting on top of it. Inside it was super; lots of staff to help with enquiries, reasonably priced souvenirs, and a model of what the whole area would eventually look like. Posters around the wall informed visitors about the local area and forthcoming events.

We went for an overpriced coffee in one of the trendy shops and then had a look along the seafront. Well we tried to but continually had to move out of the way of skateboarders. I wish this trend would die a death as it did in the early 80s. They are becoming a bloody nuisance.

The science museum around the corner looked interesting: they advertised adult evenings (what a great idea). Adults can go for a scientific play making wheels run uphill, building bridges or exploring the universe in the planetarium without getting distracted by the kids wanting to have a go!

12: Interhash 2004 Cardiff

On the way back we passed a primary school with a bizarre fence around it. The theme was nautical and it looked as though it had been designed by children. Fish and boats were painted on it as though drawn by a child. I found out later that this was exactly what had happened: the school was so fed up with the fence being vandalised that they had got the children and youths from the area to design the new fence themselves. It was a little more expensive to put up but since its erection there has been no vandalism to it at all.

Returning to the halls we met up with the rest of the Isle of Wight hash, most of whom had been setting a trail for the next day. A quick shower and we were on our way to the Millennium Stadium. We walked through the park along the banks of a babbling brook and headed down to the fairy tale castle at the bottom.

The castle was originally a wooden hill fort designed to defend a ford on the river Taff. The Romans later rebuilt it as a stone structure. It is actually possible still to see some of the Roman stones used. A section of the outer wall has been scraped away revealing the Roman construction underneath. However, in the 1800s it was rebuilt by the Marquis of Bute as a fantasy castle, a sort of mixture of a French château and a medieval home for the knights of the Round Table.

Straight across the road is the Millennium Stadium: a grand structure of tubular steel and huge counterweights that support the retractable roof. Being a sport illiterate I had never actually been to a football or Rugby stadium before. I was astonished by the size of the thing.

I went inside and saw that 5000 hashers were just lost in this magnificent edifice: a pitch in the middle; with tiered seating rising up to the roof. The first thing I noticed on the pitch was a lager tanker; the type you see on the motorway with Carling written down the side. It was placed in the centre of the stadium and there were pipes leading from it directly to the bar.

We all headed straight for the bar. It was the best Carling I have ever tasted, crisp, clear. cooled to just the right temperature, the freshest Carling you can get unless you go to the brewery. It is always wonderful how quickly you can get served at the bar; as everyone has paid in advance there is no queue, just go and grab what you fancy.

However, the food was not so well organised - the queues stretched for miles. As I waited my turn I asked Flossing where the actual grass pitch was as the floor was solid concrete. She looked at me as though I had just beamed down from the planet Zog. 'Don't you know anything about the stadium' she asked? 'I thought everyone knew that the grass is grown in a field a few miles outside Cardiff. In fact there are four pitches growing at any one time. They choose the best one then deliver it to the stadium. It is laid out for the match then taken up and returned to its field.' Well, I thought to myself, you learn something new every day.

After dinner we were all ready for a bit of a dance. Unfortunately there was no band or disco, just lots of hash acts. There was everything imaginable, song and dance routines comedians, and choirs, even a bit of poetry. However, the majority of acts involved people taking their clothes off. Snowman said he was really bored with watching all these women taking their clothes off. I agreed with him and then thought, 'what am I saying? People pay good money to watch this sort of thing!' However several hours of nudity does tend to pall after a while, so we all went for a look around the hash haberdash. There were some fantastic T shirts from the Far East with loud vibrant colours, hash jewellery, shorts, running shoes even a badge with the universal hash symbol of two feet that lit up. I bought one of those; the light emitting diodes were really bright even under the floodlights.

At last the band started up and a crowd of us took to the dance floor. It was good music and we were all really enjoying it. After half an hour they announced that the stadium was about to close but we could continue the party at nearby pubs. This resulted in large amounts of grumbling about the length of time the hash acts were on, how we had paid good money for entertainment and hadn't had any. Hyacinth and I caught a taxi back to the halls.

The next day was clear and fine; it was time to do some running. I decided to go on the IOW hash trail that was called the Goose and Cuckoo run. This started at Blenhaven and was nearly all downhill apparently. Well, it was a superb run: laid with care and dedication by Cooperman. aided by Snowman, P-rick, Stalker and Hooker. The forest tracks were wide enough for hashers to run 5 abreast. This gave the faster runners the chance to overtake and the slower ones time to relax and chat to others.

12: Interhash 2004 Cardiff

It actually was nearly all downhill, heading steadily towards the Goose and Cuckoo pub. This is a classic country pub, miles from anywhere. A tough journey down a rutted one track road by car or, across three miles of fields as the hasher flies.

It is an old white farmhouse type of building with spectacular views across the valley. The landlord had pints of real ale, freshly poured from the barrel, sitting on the bar ready for thirsty hashers. These disappeared with alacrity.

Out in the garden there was a live band that played some Jazz numbers with gusto. However, the band was not loud enough to prevent us hearing the American contingent that talked very loudly about nothing - continually.

The second half of the run was taken at a more leisurely pace; it is difficult to run with several pints of real ale inside you! There were a couple of half hearted false trails but the hash basically went down towards the canal. The downs downs seemed to go on forever. The hares all got one, as did numerous sinners. P-rick drank one with some lighted toilet tissue stuck up his bottom for some reason (don't ask) and then it was time for the coach back.

The songs on the coach were hash versions of old favourites. There was the Rolf Harris' Tiny Kangaroo Down Sport, which became Tie My Kangaroo Down Sport.. but I won't print any more.

Then there was the Yogi Bear song to the tune of doo dar doo dar day. The song was something to do with Yogi and his Dick, cheese, cucumbers and various other 'subtle' associations. I wont print those words either. However I am sure you get the general idea.

We arrived back at halls and headed for the kitchen. Coffee was definitely on the agenda. Throbbin Hood from Cheltenham Men Only H3 had just boiled the kettle and we shared his water. MOH3 is very keen on singing; they have their own song book produced by Deep Throat, a hasher from Blue yonder. It contains a classic range of popular songs including Bohemian Rhapsody, Beatles numbers and lots of hash songs like the ones above.

MOH3 go on tour every couple of years; in 2003 they went to Italy. Standing in St Marks Square they got out the guitar and started to sing about a little green frog. They all have terrific voices and harmonise superbly. Apparently within a few minutes people were coming up to them and giving money. They tried to explain that they just sang for fun but could not convince people not to keep throwing money at them. They all wore white jackets and panama hats. They walked in step with military precision and hummed the theme from the Godfather whenever they went into a bar or restaurant. Then they would burst into song this was all taken with excellent humour by the restaurant owners who appreciated the impromptu cabaret. Some of the other customers clapped them all when they finished singing.

Throbbin Hood said it was wonderful to have people welcome a group of British lads into bars and not to be tainted with the reputation of being hooligans. The hash should become ambassadors for the United Nations.

Throbbin had gone on the Gower peninsular run on Friday and said it was fun if a little long. There was an American guy on the coach with them who was the spitting image of Bill Clinton. Every time he stood up the MOH3 group all hummed the American national anthem then said "I did not have sexual relations with that women." By the time they were on the coach coming back the guy would not move from his chair.

The evening was spent at the stadium again. This time they had opened up far more food places and we all got served very quickly. The video from Interhash two years ago at Goa was playing on the TV screens. We all had fun trying to spot Poor Sod and Flossing who had been filmed extensively on one of the runs. Sadly they must have ended up on the cutting room floor as there was no sign of them.

The hash acts were again in full swing so we all got bored watching people take their clothes off. Then a local mayor decided to come and talk to us all. This was brave, to say the least. She was introduced by GBH the Cardiff hasher responsible for organising the whole event. She stood up said, "Welcome to Cardiff" and there was a cheer and calls for her to get her tits out! She then said she had never heard of hashers before but could tell they liked to party. She thought it was a super combination getting fit with a run, then relaxing with a beer.

Next came a Welsh Male Voice Choir. They were superb if a little non PC. I think that singing I Vow to Thee My Country followed by Land of Hope and Glory, with nationalities from all over the world present, was perhaps, a little insensitive; but there you go. Jerusalem went down well as did Guide me Oh Thou Great Redeemer.

12: Interhash 2004 Cardiff

The band and disco then started in earnest and a great night was had on the dance floor. I went to the bar for a drink and was talking to some of the Scandinavian hashers who were still trying to drum up support for their Silver Jubilee Hash. They told me about the Helsinki Hash House Harriers who have a mixed sauna after every run. They go running around Helsinki have some down downs and then all pile into the sauna. Apparently they welcome visitors, especially at the Hole in the Ice Hash.

This involves a weekend affair in February with runs, followed by a few beers. They all go into the sauna, then run out naked across a frozen river; they then climb into a hole cut into the ice! I said 'The water must be freezing don't you get any heart attacks.' They said 'Not so far, but we would not recommend it for anyone with a heart condition.'

We all had a great time dancing to the disco and the bands. Hyacinth and I headed off back home about 1 pm but Hooker and a few others continued on a crawl round the pubs and clubs of Cardiff. In the morning Hooker was a little worse for wear. He had apparently been snogging a woman he met in one of the pubs and had arranged to meet her the next night. Unfortunately he had no memory of the snogging or of where he had arranged to meet her. 'Alcohol provokes the desire but takes away the performance' and the memory!

The next day Hyacinth and I decided to go on the walk around Cardiff. I could not face more coach travel. We walked around the park, down the river bank, through some woods onto a village on the outskirts of Cardiff. We returned by bus and got off in the Central Park for down downs. It was supposed to be a gentle 3 mile stroll; it turned out to be a 5 mile hike. The hares then got out some beers for down downs. He asked if there were any Germans on the hash. About ten people stood up. Right he said you are going to play a game called aeroplanes please put your hands out straight and fly around the circle as though you are an aeroplane. Make sure you make appropriate noises like neeow. They all started flying about the field. The hare then got some of the English hashers to follow them singing the Damn Busters theme and going neeer daka daka daka until all the German planes were shot down!

This was followed by the Irish mine sweepers. All the Irish hashers were told to put their fingers in their ears and feel in front of them with their feet so they could clear the minefield. We then all sang

'Father Abraham'. I knew what was going to happen so I stood well back. Hyacinth stood at the front and was soaked with beer as it was thrown over everyone during the chorus. The atmosphere was super, it was all taken in good humour and the relaxed fun loving approach to life that is hashing.

Chapter 13

Havenstreet Station Run

It was a cold December morning when a small pack assembled at Havenstreet railway station. This is a steam railway station situated in a village just outside Ryde called, surprisingly enough, Havenstreet. The steam railway is only about 5 miles in length running along some of the old tracks that Beeching destroyed in the 1960s. It is maintained by a group of volunteers who take great pride in running an efficient service that links perfectly with the Island's actual rail network at Smallbrook junction.

The Island's main rail network is now just one track that runs from Ryde to Shanklin. It has rolling stock consisting of 1923 underground trains that surprisingly still run. The real trains are probably not much younger than those run by the steam enthusiasts who wish to preserve the past.

Havenstreet is a wonderful place to visit; the station is kept as it would have looked in the Victorian era with a waiting room, museum and even a carriage that Queen Victoria once travelled in. On a sunny afternoon it has a relaxing family atmosphere with people picnicking on the grass as steam trains stop to pick up passengers. There is

Granny Winters Café and a children's playground. The roundtrip from end to end, Wootton to Smallbrook only takes about half and hour. The shop has lots of rail memorabilia, including Thomas the Tank Engine, by the sack full. It is a lovely friendly place where people can really relax.

However, on October the 31st it is taken over by the Bellevue Players, a local drama group in Ryde, and we convert it to a much more sinister place. The pleasant warm family atmosphere is changed to a place of horror and suspense for Halloween Ghost Walks. The public address system has tracks of ghostly sounds and screaming played at high volume. The signals have dead bodies hanging from them and there are skeletons and pumpkins glowing eerily in the foggy evening. The trains also look very atmospheric with the steam coming out into the night air as they cool down. Alien electric blue light illuminates the signal box; the sort of blue light that would not look out of place in a Stephen Spielberg film. The Victorian carriages have no electricity so the only light inside comes from the oil lamps we carry, as we tell our tales of ghosts and ghouls.

It is astonishingly popular, with over 800 people coming to see the show over the three evenings it is on. It normally begins with the people waiting in the queue being accosted by a priest who warns them not to venture beyond the gate. He then starts talking to a vampire who explains that he is looking for a virgin and a drink. The priests suggests that some of the members of the audience may be able to help him and he then goes and sucks the blood out of the neck of a young girl (she is a plant - one of the actors pretending to be an audience member) who is waiting in the queue. This causes much consternation among those waiting to come in.

We move the audience into the railway station, and actors in period costume guide them on towards the museum. Usually at this point, just as the audience are relaxing, we have what is called a grumbler. This is an actor dressed as a monster who runs out of a concealed alleyway and straight towards the audience, usually brandishing his battleaxe and screaming at the top of his voice. It scares the living daylights out of everyone, even those in the cast who are expecting it.

The museum is at the back of the railway shop and it is full of old lamps, signalling equipment and documents and maps to do with the railway when it was first built. It has one very important feature:

13: Heavenstreet Station Run

there are no windows in it and when the lights are turned off it is so dark that you cannot see your hand in front of your face. This is useful in a ghost walk; we bring the crowd into the room and turn the light off; a disembodied voice then tells a ghostly tale and sound effects are used at the appropriate moments. Suddenly, out of the darkness, a skeleton will appear. Strange ghostly shapes float above the heads of those present. It is all very disorienting and quite frightening, at least for the children.

We move on to the carriages. These can only hold 20 people each so we have to split the group up into three. 'This group is the Vampires what are you called?' 'Vampires' they respond. The same for the Werewolves and the Ghoulies. Of course we have to instruct the Werewolves not get tangled up with the Ghoulies as it could be most unpleasant.

In one carriage there is David Philo, a terrific chap and a talented actor; 70 years of age but he could give Christopher Lee a run for his money. He is sitting down dressed as a vampire as the audience comes in. He doesn't say a word for five minutes just sitting in silence and letting the tension build up. Then he tells a story about how vampires have been misrepresented in the media and that they are nice really. At this point Mike Bauldry, another stalwart of the drama group, dressed as Van Helsing, comes rushing through the door with a cross and a wooden stake. 'Ah! foul fiend, I have found you!' he says and proceeds to bang the stake through the vampires heart, to much screaming from the vampire and the audience.

In the next carriage up there is a tale being told of a haunting; whenever the ghost appeared there was a smell of lavender. Jane, who is very slim and really is the person who keeps Bellevue going with her enthusiasm and dedication, is actually hiding under one of the chairs with a bottle of lavender spray producing the odour at the appropriate moments. Eventually she appears from her hiding place, jumping out between the legs of an unsuspecting member of the audience.

The third carriage contains Interloper and myself. We have set up a coffin with a 'dead' body at one end and a ouija board at the other end. No one seemed to want to sit down at the end with the dead body for some reason and they were not keen on being near the ouija board either.

Our tale was about a young girl called Maria, murdered on her wedding night. She was forced to marry the local squire of Havenstreet, Sir Nicholas. However, she wanted to marry young Tom her true love from childhood. She is found dead outside the nuptial chamber. We explain to all those present that inside the coffin are the last mortal remains of Maria and that tonight we are going to perform a séance to contact Maria and find out who killed her. We tell the audience to join hands and repeat the words, 'Is anybody there?' They all join in, if a little reluctantly.

We place a finger each on to the golden goblet and, behold it moves across the Ouija board. 'Is there anybody there?' 'Is that you Maria?' The answer comes out 'YES'; the goblet now moving without us touching it. Hidden under the table is my 12-year-old son with a bloody big magnet. However, this seemed to freak out one or two people who decided to leave the carriage. It is very dark and the mist outside gives everything a spooky atmosphere.

The questions continue and eventually it is revealed that Sir Nicholas is the murderer. 'Where is he Maria?' HERE is spelt out. 'What is his intent?' DEATH is spelt, then BEWARE HE COMES! At this point Sir Nicholas charges in through the door with a huge knife. At the same time the dead body of Maria sits bolt upright and starts screaming. I have never seen people jump out of their seats and scream so much themselves. Sir Nicholas proceeds to stab us both to death with lots of blood pouring from the knife. Then he warns all present not to reveal what occurred here tonight or they will suffer a similar fate.

As they walked out I overheard two members of the audience warning their friends not to bring the children inside. 'It is very frightening' they said. This of course meant the children were desperate to see it. I suppose it is a bit like watching Dr Who as a child. You are frightened of the Daleks but do not want to miss the episode. Children do enjoy being scared.

The audience would then go on to walk past chained up monsters that appeared to be eating maggots and throwing them over passing people. The maggots are really left squirming in the tray and what is thrown is some cooked pasta! It looks fairly gross though!

At the end we smoked a witch at the stake. She was supposed to be burnt but we could not figure out how to do the flames and just used a smoke machine. The grand finale was a couple of us singing the

13: Heavenstreet Station Run

Monster Mash and the rest of the cast dancing around in monster outfits. It was great fun and done as an amateur dramatic presentation; all profits to the Bellevue players and Havenstreet railway.

However, it was astonishing how much money was made; over £1800 in three nights. I must be in the wrong profession - it takes a month to make that in my day job. There seems to be a huge appetite for live entertainment. At the moment there is nothing on television but soap operas and reality TV shows: decorating, gardening, cooking, Big Brother type stuff. What has happened to all the great comedies of the past, Porridge, Blackadder, Only Fools and Horses. Where are all the action adventure series of the seventies? There is nothing on TV like The Sweeny! Where are all the actors employed? You obviously don't need actors to do reality TV. You don't need much money either. It is cheap, and that is probably why there is so much of the rubbish about! And, a question close to my heart, will the BBC ever bring out a new series of Blake's Seven?

Moving back to the present, the run went across the road from Havenstreet station car park and headed into Combley woods. It was cold, damp and misty. The atmosphere was wonderful, as the pack seemed to run in silence, the sound deadened by the soft leaves underfoot and the heavy air. It was heading up hill. Strangely, it didn't appear to be, until you wondered why you were out of breath and looked back along the path. I stopped running and walked the rest of the way to the top. One of my rules is never run up steep hills, walk to the top, then run down the other side to catch up. Mongrel joined me and told me about her recent trip to London. She was travelling up with a few friends to do some girly shopping. As she got on the train she found it was incredibly crowded so they all decided to upgrade to first class. When they got into the first class carriage there were a couple of people reading their papers sitting by the window. Apart from that they had the whole carriage to themselves.

They were in high spirits and a little noisy, discussing in loud voices what had happened over the last week and explaining to one of the group what hashing was all about.

Mongrel then started talking about how fantastic The Phantom of the Opera is. She explained about the chandelier almost crashing down on top of the audience and the wonderful boat effects. She then did an impression of the singing. 'In sleep he sang to me, in dreams he came, that voice which calls to me, and speaks my name' etc As she sang this, very badly, there was some movement between the two people reading their papers. She couldn't see their faces but she got the impression they were laughing at her. Not that it bothered her - she just carried on. A few stops later the people reading the papers got up to leave the carriage; one of them was a very amused looking Andrew Lloyd Webber!

We ran on through the trees and headed down into the valley. At the bottom was a fast running stream. The ground was slippery and we skidded our way along the track, avoiding low tree branches and trying to stop falling into the water. It was to no avail - the trail led into the stream; it was cold and wet. Tanglefoot (75 years of age but she runs like a gazelle on speed) gingerly stepped in and said 'It may be freezing but at least it has got a nice firm bottom.' 'Sex sex sex it is all you women think about' said a passing runner!

We went back to the White Heart pub Havenstreet. This is a well run country; pub the landlord is very welcoming and he keeps the beer beautifully. He has an unusual menu, which is not to my taste, but those who have eaten there say the food is terrific. The down downs were done outside so we didn't upset the regulars. Wheerzee was given one for exhausting J on the on in. 'I can't stretch my legs any further he has completely exhausted me she said!' And Stalker got one for disbelieving On On calls. It's this way, Oh no it isn't, Oh yes it is etc.

Chapter 14

Seaview Dog Day Run

Travelling down the coast from Ryde in an Easterly direction you will eventually come to Seaview, a quaint village full of rich yachties. Poor Sod lives on the main Puckpool to Seaview coast road. He used to share with BT but since she has gone travelling around the world he is now on his own. He probably misses the dogs in the freezer!

Mongrel lives in the upstairs flat. I asked her if I could pop in and use her facilities. When I came out of the loo I found I was locked in and the hash had already disappeared. I opened the window and called out, telling the world I was locked in. No one responded. Great, I thought, I'll be trapped here until they return. I tried to phone Mongrel on her mobile; it was turned off, of course. Then Mongrel appeared from round the corner where she had been hiding all the time. She found the whole thing most amusing and couldn't stop laughing as she opened the door. I vowed to get my revenge!

We caught up with the hash that were checking down the road. It was a glorious sunny day. with a view across the Solent to Portsmouth, uninterrupted by any haze. The sky was azure blue and this was reflected in the water. Gentle waves lapped in as we ran on the beach, a mixture of shingle and sand.

The Portsmouth Millennium Tower was clearly visible across the water a huge white structure with a viewing platform at the top. Now complete (2005) but not yet open. We have been told it will cost £5 to go up if you want to walk up the hundreds of steps but £7 to go by lift. It is hoped that it will be as successful as the Eiffel tower. I will certainly be going up it, as the view should be breathtaking (Well, what you have left, after climbing the steps!).

There was a good pack of about 30 hashers all ready for the off and we guessed the trail would lead East toward Seaview Central and not west towards Ryde where the running is limited. We set off at a cracking pace along the road looking at the view and avoiding grockles* who tended to block up the pavements.

On the right there are bungalows, many with nautical themes in their names. Gull Sands, Shearwater, Roger the Cabin Boy, well that sort of thing! On the left there are new sea defences, solid concrete, buttressed by huge rocks placed on the beach.

How they actually got the rocks there is a mystery to me. Some of them are the size of a large bungalow and must weigh tons. There is also a sea overflow tunnel built under the road that directs the water into a salt marsh at the back of the bungalows rather than flooding the road.

We continued to the end of Seaview Toll road and then went up public footpath number R95 towards Springvale and on past the Roadside Inn pub. We turned up Nettlestone hill and ran round the back towards a plush Hotel. The hotel food is apparently nouveau cuisine. I have heard this consists of exotic salad leaves, small amounts of meat and the price tag of a small Volkswagen. Once you have eaten there you are broke and still hungry.

The trail went along winding public footpaths under dappled sunshine for a couple of miles. There was then a check at a junction where a large pool of muddy water had accumulated. Tanoy headed straight for the middle of the pool and stood there looking around for a viable target. Several of us stood there transfixed as if by a snake. We knew she was about to splash everyone but we just stood and waited for it to happen.

Derogatory Isle of Wight term for tourists

14: Seaview Dog Day Run

Within seconds there were sheets of muddy water heading in our direction. We all jumped back, at last released from the hypnotic trance. It was to no avail, we were covered in mud and foul water. Mongrel ran to the pool and joined in. They were both so involved in splashing in a 360-degree circumference that they did not notice the party of Dutch tourists walking up the path opposite.

Calls of 'Civilians on the track! Stop splashing' were lost in the general screaming and questioning of Tanoy's parentage.

The people coming up the track were serious Dutch walkers in immaculate hiking gear and pristine walking jackets. They all carried ordinance survey maps and compasses.

Two of them were covered in mud the second they walked around the corner. The look of astonishment on their faces had to be seen to be believed. The astonishment quickly changed to cold fury and this at last stopped Tanoy in her tracks. She apologised and begged for forgiveness. This had little effect, they were still really annoyed.

She eventually got down on her knees and offered to kiss their feet in recompense. This sort of broke the ice and they started to see the funny side of it all. Tanoy was as good as her word and kissed their muddy boots.

We waved goodbye on semi-friendly terms and headed on down the trail. Within a couple of hundred metres we realised it was a false trail and had to turn around and run past our Dutch friends again. The trail continued on towards St Helens along a nicely paved track. Several false trails delayed us so when we eventually turned off towards the sea and St Helens bay, guess who was in front of us. Yes, the Dutch contingent, who looked around as if a bunch of lunatics were stalking them.

We arrived at St Helens Bay and stopped for a breather by the tower of the old church. This dilapidated structure sits at the top of the beach by the high water mark. There was a half-hearted attempt by Poor Sod to get us on a false trail towards Bembridge. However, we had been running for an hour and a half and we knew it was at least another half an hour to get back. Everyone turned west and headed along the beach towards Seaview.

It was now a glorious day and there were crowds of sunbathers on the beach and even one or two braving the water. The beach is mainly sand and shingle; on the left there are gently sloping hills with a profusion of trees on the top. The trail led up into the trees but I knew there was no way out.

I stuck to the beach and let the energetic ones climb up and down the cliffs. Mongrel showed no inclination to climb the hills and was walking along in front of J and me. We decided it was the ideal time to throw Mongrel into the sea. I needed to get her back for locking me in, and it is a general rule that the hare goes for a dip if there is water around.

Sensing our intent as we came up behind her, she was off like a whippet. We gave chase but couldn't get close. However, we were in for a war of attrition and continued to shadow her at a distance. Eventually the gap was closed and after a game of British Bulldog she was grabbed and taken to the shore. Lots of abuse came our way; she was struggling and kicking, all to no avail. We then slowly lowered her into the water. Revenge is a dish best served cold; the sea is very cold in April!

We continued along the beach to Priory Bay. This is a glorious spot just below the Priory Bay Hotel. It is a long, sandy beach with shallow water between two natural groynes of rock. If you don't know it's there, it is very hard to find when the tide is in. To discover it, a good climb over slippery rocks is required. However it is worth the effort as Priory is quieter than Seagrove bay beach, which is next door, and the shallow water is ideal for children. I have been there on a weekday in July and had the whole beach to myself.

We climbed the rocks and arrived on Seagrove beach, some of the hash checked up Gully road, this is a very steep hill leading from the top of the beach and going back the way we had come an hour ago. It is mainly used as a slipway to get boats on the beach. At the bottom end of Gully road, where the beach begins, there is a tiny café called The Bay cafe. This seems to be just an ice cream and sandwich place at first but in the summer they do evening fish suppers on the beach. You can order what you would like the day before and it is caught fresh for you the next day. It is then cooked that very evening - Sea Bass, Crab or Lobster to name just a few of the delicacies. It is fabulous - fish straight from the sea tastes completely different from the frozen fare we are used to. Give it a go!

14: Seaview Dog Day Run

Most of us stayed on the beach and continued to Ryde. We ran along the sand and then had to go onto the road at Seaview as the beach ends at a headland. We jogged past the Seaview Yacht Club where there was a large crowd sitting in the sun and drinking, but virtually no one sailing, sounds like my type of exercise!

A very welcome ON IN sign (written in flour on the ground; it means go this way for beer) showed us the way back to Poor Sod's place were the hash barbeque was already firing up. There were enough sausages and burgers to feed the five thousand and plenty of wine was flowing. We sat on the beach, caught some rays, ate some food and drank some wine. Oddball would have approved!

Chapter 15

Eurohash 2005 Amsterdam

It was a bright, clear morning on the 9th of August 2005 as Cooperman, Snowman and I set off for Eurohash. We caught the 9.30 ferry from Fishbourne to Portsmouth and arrived bang on time at 10.15am. We decided to drive up the A3 towards London and then go round the M25 and down the M20 to Dover. We all had bitter memories of trying to get to Dover along the south coast road. On paper it looks much shorter but there are lots of towns, traffic lights and roundabouts. The last time I took the coast route it took me six hours to get to Dover and I missed the ferry.

The A3 was clear as a bell as was the M25 (astonishing!) We arrived in Dover at 2pm and were told we could get on the 2.30pm ferry even though we were booked on the 3.30pm, fantastic!

The ferry was the Pride of Calais a standard clone of all the P and O ferries, even having the same international food court restaurant as the ones that go from Portsmouth. Snowman and I were a little peckish so we went to get some food. Cooperman had brought a picnic hamper with what looked like enough food to last him the entire week.

Competition seems to have improved the ferries; there was no queuing and the food was reasonably priced. I had chicken casserole, a drink and desert for about a fiver. We watched the white cliffs of Dover slide into the distance; one hour and fifteen minutes later we were docking at Calais.

The cost of this 22-mile journey for three of us, plus a car was £40 each. I feel I must compare this with the cost of getting one person and a car off the Isle of Wight and over the four miles to Portsmouth - £70! There is something wrong somewhere.

Miss Belgium, no not a beauty contest but a bit of lifestyle advice! We did not want to stop in Belgium if it possibly could be avoided. We would either stop at the French border and camp for the night or drive like men possessed for the Dutch border.

As it was we arrived at the French border in plenty of time to drive across Belgium before nightfall. The second part of the plan involved a campsite with a late bar near to a lovely town with delicious cheap moules and quality wine.

Belgium is flat and seems to consist of ugly industrial estates interspersed with wind turbines. I know from experience that the food and drink on the motorway is expensive and disgusting. I also know that they ritually sacrifice any outsiders after sunset. (Ok I just made that up but I am not going to take any chances) We drove on along a motorway paved with good intentions, heading into a sudden dark squall of rain that only seemed to be on the Belgian side of the border.

I decided to lighten the sense of unease by putting on a compilation of 60s and 70s music. We all sang along to Queen, Lou Reed and Supertramp. Cooperman even translated the words of Je t'aime; apparently she wants him to enter her kidneys - at least that is what it sounded like to Coops.

Cooperman gave us a fascinating little anecdote about Jane Birken, the women who sings in je t'aime. She was a pupil at Upper Chine School, Shanklin, Isle of Wight. They do not seem to advertise this fact when they talk about past Alumni - I can't understand why!

It was heading towards 5.30pm when, with a sigh of relief, we crossed the border and entered Holland. We immediately started looking for a campsite. The first town we came to was called Sluis (pronounced slice) and they seemed to have a festival on. Cooperman asked at the tourist information place for a campsite, then directed us

15: Eurohash 2005 Amsterdam

with unerring accuracy to a wonderful spot just on the edge of town. Snowman spotted the sign and we had found our home for the night.

The ground was soft and easy to put pegs in so we set up our tents and headed for the bar. A couple of pints later we were ready to find some food. Snowman asked the campsite owner if we could get moules anywhere. 'Oh no problem' he said. 'Everywhere does them; in fact they are particularly large and juicy at the moment.' This sounded very positive so we walked across the road and into town.

The place was stunning, with traditional Dutch houses, clean and prosperous looking. There was a canal that split the high street in two, and people were out on it in rowing boats. There were several bands playing and, in particular, there was a Beatles tribute group who were excellent. It was heaving with crowds of people doing some serious retail therapy and listening to the bands. The first couple of restaurants we tried were very busy with waiting times ranging from two hours up to when Belgium freezes over. We went down a side street and found an oldie worldy type place that had plenty of seats and moules on the menu. The moules were delicious, large and tasty, and they came with enough frites to sink a barge. It was all washed down with cold beers and the whole meal was only 14 pounds each. Fantastic!

We went for a walk around town; listened to a few Beatles numbers and returned to the campsite feeling all was well with the world. The site bar was still open at midnight so we had a game of pool and further refreshment.

The next day we studied the map and decided to try going on the scenic route off the motorway.

However, the problem with rural Holland is tractors. We seemed to be plagued with the things. After five minutes on the road a tractor appeared in front of us: impossible to pass, and averaging the same speed as an arthritic snail. After an hour of frustration and a total distance of ten miles covered, we gave up the country roads and headed back to the motorway.

Our progress was much improved and by two o'clock we were on the outskirts of Amsterdam. We decided to drive to Uitgeest where the castle for Eurohash was situated. Apparently we could get a train into Amsterdam for our 2 day Prelube. The railway parking at Uitgeest looked very dodgy so I asked at the local garage if it would be safe to leave the car there overnight. 'Not if you want to see it again' said the helpful assistant.

Well, we had to drive up the line a bit to Heemskirk. This looked more like Peckham than the Bronx; still not ideal, but it would have to do. We caught a basic commuter train that seemed to stop at every possible station and a few times for no apparent reason at all. It took about 45 minutes to reach Amsterdam and during this time we tried as hard as possible to pay our fare.

We searched along the carriages as far as the locked doors at either end. We asked other passengers where we could find the guard. 'Oh, he may be along later, or he may not' said one helpful lady. I assumed that Amsterdam would be like a London station. If you got off in London Waterloo without a ticket, you could be shot; or locked up in Guantanamo Bay forever.

As we got off at Amsterdam Central I went looking for a guard, driver or just anyone in a uniform to pay for our tickets. I eventually found someone who looked vaguely like a railway employee and asked where I could pay for my ticket. He looked at me as though I was mad and walked on. We then walked down the platform for about 200 yards where there was a set of steps that led onto the street. No barriers, guard dogs, barbed wire or armed police to take your money, I gave up and followed Coops and Snowman down. Snowman commented on how he recognised the outside of the station from the film Puppet on a Chain and was expecting to see a speedboat driven by Patrick Allen appear around the bend any second.

I had no idea where the hotel was as I had booked it on the Internet and was only interested in its price and the fact it was connected to a curry house. We got a taxi and then wished that we hadn't - even the taxi driver told us it would have been easier to walk. There were lots of roads closed, stationary traffic stretching back to Belgium and a serious one-way system. What would have been a five-minute walk became a twenty-minute taxi journey.

We eventually arrived, about 500 yards from the station, on the side of a canal just across the bridge from Hotel Viaja. What we did not realise until the taxi driver mentioned it was that the hotel was in the middle of the red light district.

15: Eurohash 2005 Amsterdam

Just around the corner were the ladies of the night – well, in this case the day, standing in the sort of underwear that invited a chill. They would smile and wave at any passing man. Then they started pouting and revealing enough bare flesh to make a grown hasher blush; we hurried past to our hotel entrance.

Well, we settled in to our rooms. I had an interesting view out of the window of scantily dressed young ladies and lots of bars. We met outside sitting on the side of the canal and drinking grand beers. It was just lovely, the setting sun reflecting off the water of the canal, cold beer, boats chugging gently past, the windows full of enough hard core pornography and vibrators to make your eyes water!

We really were starting to relax and drink in the atmosphere. A second beer followed the first, then a third to keep them both company. We went for a walk in search of food and eventually ended up in the curry house attached to the hotel (they did discount for hotel guests). It wasn't bad for a curry house on the European mainland, still not of Bradford or Birmingham quality but a thousand times better than Arhus. The discount sort of disappeared apparently; we were given it but we couldn't figure out how from the bill. Never mind, the price was reasonable and we all had three more beers so were not in the mood for arguing higher mathematics such as percentage discounts.

It was time to go and investigate Cocoas the Australian bar that was to be the venue for Eurohash 2005. It advertised itself on the hash website as 'Cocoas Australian bar, lousy food and warm beer'. It also stated that Cocoas had promised cheap beer for the hash providing the strip pool competition took place again. This competition had started last year at the 'Far Canal Hash'. If you lose at a game of pool you strip off your clothes; it would certainly be an incentive to improve your potting skills.

We wandered down the side of the canal using our portable satellite navigation system called Cooperman. He looked at the map of Amsterdam once and knew the way to anywhere, even in the dark. What it must be to have a photographic memory!

Cocoas was a great place: large, comfortable and fairly deserted when we arrived. After about half an hour a few hashers started to appear. Pussy Galore introduced us to a couple of brothers, Silver Fox (because of his silver rather than grey hair) and Big Balls (because of some large oval things) who were making a bid for Interhash in Perth. They were typical Ausies, taking the rise out of each other continually; in fact we just refereed and enjoyed their quick wit.

Pussy said if any of us wanted to try some marijuana then there was a hash café just across the square. Usually if the Dutch host Eurohash you get some marijuana in your goody bag so you get some hash from the hash. Not this year apparently, you had to buy your own. Well I thought I must have a look at this and try the experience of a real hash café.

Pussy introduced me to a fellow English hasher who will remain anonymous and we wandered across to the hash café. My companion said she had always wanted to try some hash but was not able to because of her job. She was regularly drug tested at work any trace of marijuana in her system and she would be instantly sacked.

This seems totally unreasonable, as what she does in her private life really should have nothing to do with her job, especially when she is taking the stuff in a country where it is not illegal to do so. (She was currently between jobs, so felt she could give it a go). However, this is nothing compared to what is happening in America. Over there some companies have introduced a system called TADS.

TADS stands for tobacco alcohol and drugs – a policy adopted by some companies in America. It makes the taking of drugs, the consumption of alcohol or the smoking of cigarettes prohibited activities for their employees.

This is not just while at work but at any time in your life. If you are an employee of one of these companies you are not allowed to drink or smoke at any time. This means that if you are at home during the weekend and you drink a half pint of beer on a Saturday night, you can be sacked by your employer. These rules are enforced by random urine checks of employees. Who said slavery has been abolished?

Let's hope it doesn't happen over here or drinking on a hash will only be done by those with a UB40.

At the end of the bar in the hash cafe was a glass-covered table with every possible type of marijuana on sale. There was black, brown, sleeper, Lebanese and all kinds of other little oxo cube type blocks to

15: Eurohash 2005 Amsterdam

choose from. There were also some seeds and even some stuff that looked like dried grass in a little packet (hence the name I guess).

I asked what the difference was between them. The guy selling them (drug dealer I suppose) explained it was a question of strength; he said the ones at the top were the strong ones and the ones below the weaker ones. I asked him how they compared to the stuff that was available 25 years ago. He said they didn't; even the weakest he sold was three times stronger than what was available then. My companion went for the weakest stuff and retired to a table at the back to try rolling a joint - not an easy thing to do if you are not used to it. I tried to help but created something that looked like a piece of soggy toilet tissue with stringy brown bits hanging out.

I gave up at this point and just stayed with the beer. An expert Dutchman came over to help her roll a joint and created some perfect specimens almost instantly. Apparently the feeling is much more subtle than alcohol, it makes you relax and feel like talking bollocks to anyone who will listen. Actually it sounds a lot like alcohol to me!

The next day was going to have a cultural element. Snowman and I decided to go on the canal trip to find out about the city. We started our trip on the Amstel river: this was dammed to create the name Amsterdam and hence the city. We were told that Amsterdam is the capital of Holland, not The Haigh as I thought. Apparently Amsterdam is the second biggest port in the world, the largest being Rotterdam. The Dutch really do know how to do ship unloading. It is cheaper to dock at Rotterdam and drive a cargo across to Britain (including the cost of the channel tunnel) rather than dock at some English ports (sounds a bit bizarre to me).

The architecture in Amsterdam is all about making the buildings tall and making them thin - houses were taxed on their width when they were built. There is one house that is only 1 metre wide and 5 metres deep it must have very narrow beds in the bedrooms. We went past the entrance to the expensive Gentleman's Canal where you can see seven bridges almost hiding behind each other as they go into the distance. There is the skinny bridge, so called because the builders ran out of money and made it as basic as possible without actually collapsing.

In the 1960s Amsterdam Council decided to put up small fences around all the canals to stop cars from driving into the water. This was hugely expensive costing 100s of guilders a metre. There are 100 canals and about 1000 bridges. Even now with the fence firmly in place there is, on average, one car a week that ends up in the water.

We passed a beautiful wooden trading ship, an exact replica of an East Indian trading company boat from the last century. Unemployed people had volunteered to build it as a sort of job creation scheme and a way of learning new skills. It was absolutely stunning with three masts to hold the sails and six cannon ports on each side. Painted in blue and yellow, with ornate figureheads at the front and back, it certainly seemed a better way to while away the hours of unemployment than watching Trisha: this was a work of art, something to be proud of!

The Sea Palace, a floating Chinese restaurant, looked impressive until we were told that it was based on the one floating in Hong Kong harbour called the Jumbo. The Sea Palace could seat up to 700 people, the Jumbo in Hong Kong could seat 5000. That must be worth seeing!

The central station is built on an artificial island. This does not become apparent until you look on a map and realise there is no way into the station except across a bridge. It must be one of the only stations serving a capital city that is on an island.

Around about 5pm we made our way back to the hotel to get ready for the red dress run. Just as we arrived at reception Flossing and Mongrel appeared, closely followed by Poor Sod and Carol.

We had lots of hugs and did the usual questions about how the journey was. They felt it was an interesting location and that Navigator was a pervert for choosing a hotel in the middle of the red light district. I didn't waste my breath trying to explain it was booked on the Internet and I had no idea where it was; no one would believe me anyway!

We went up to get changed into our red dresses and said we would meet at the bar outside at 6pm. I had a very slinky red top and skirt plus the compulsory comical breasts to give the whole thing a mature feel!

Amsterdam must be one of the few cities in the world where you can walk out of your hotel dressed as a women in a bright red dress and nobody bats an eyelid.

15: Eurohash 2005 Amsterdam

A group of us, all visions in bright red, sat at the bar outside and we might as well have well have been invisible for the notice anyone paid us. We all had a couple of wet ones and headed to Cocoas; the place was heaving with red clad, hairy legged, fat hashers and those were just the girls!

Pussy welcomed us all onto the DIVA red dress run and off we went at a sprint down the main road. It always astonishes me how hashers can drink several pints of beer then set off at a cracking pace; in fact they continued this cracking pace for miles.

The first break we had was a check at the Rijksmuseum at least two miles away. This is a huge edifice that contains amongst other things, Rembrandt's Night Watch. I went to see it a few years ago with Hyacinth and I was astonished. I really am not normally one for spending hours in art galleries; I usually do a quick tour and say very nice now let's go to the pub?

The Night Watch was different. I walked into the room where it was and just stopped dead 'Bloody Hell' I said but very quietly as the place was like a hallowed area of a cathedral with everyone speaking in whispers. The painting is enormous covering a whole wall; the lighting gives it an eerie glow as if it is lit from within by the paint itself. I stood transfixed for ten minutes just staring in awe; the characters seemed ready to step out of the canvas into the room. It wasn't just me - everyone was staring as they walked through the door, looks of rapture on the faces as though having a religious experience (or possibly an orgasm). Either way it was worth the entrance fee on its own.

We regrouped outside the museum and got whipped by one of the Diva girls who was dressed as a dominatrix. On we ran at a ridiculous speed. I was ready to drop but had to keep up. I had no idea of the way back and really didn't want to get lost in the back streets of Amsterdam wearing a bright red dress and comical boobs. Then again I could possibly have made a bit of holiday spending money!

Eventually we arrived at Vondelpark for the beer stop. This was welcome in terms of the rest but also was good because of bursting bladders. It was not possible to find a bush without a red clad hasher hiding behind it. I must say the girls are a lot better at going to the loo alfresco when wearing a dress than the boys. I didn't seem to have enough hands to hold everything out of the way and not fall over.

After a quick hash flash (photograph) we continued through the park where families were taking in the evening air and children were playing on swings. We did actually get one or two strange looks from people as several hundred red dresses went past all shouting On On! The police then arrived and asked us what we were doing. The organiser explained it was a charity run by the Hash House Harriers; this satisfied them and we were allowed to continue.

We came out of the park and instantly got lost in a maze of streets and a shopping centre. The pack split to the four winds and I ended up with a slow moving group who had the same navigation skills as the average lemming. We walked for ages, not having a clue where we were going. However, using more luck than judgement, we eventually got back to Cocoas and collapsed in a heap.

The place was buzzing, red dresses everywhere, music blasting out, hashers dancing wildly, Mongrel and Floss dancing on top of the tables, Twonk falling over. In the side room I spotted the dentist's chair, which is a little like a medieval torture device designed to give down downs to sinners. There were lots of 'volunteers' waiting to sit down and have beer poured down their throat. I avoided this 'pleasure' and went for a more sedate beer at the bar. Silver Fox and Big balls were there, still taking the mick out of each other and accosting every passing hasher to get some pledge money for their Interhash bid.

By 2am I was ready for bed; the party was showing no sign of abating - most of them were still in full party mode. Snowman and I decided we had had enough and wandered back to our salubrious hotel. The local streets were even more bizarre in the dark, lots of new windows had appeared and there were hundreds of tourists just walking past the ladies of the night and staring in. The whole thing was surreal!

The next day I woke bright and early about 9am and went down for breakfast. Everyone was already sitting down tucking into cheese and bread, cereal and orange juice; it was very nice, and the vitamin C was welcome. We all decided to go and visit the flower market: I know it seems a bit girly but why not. We walked for about a mile and came to a very tacky market selling some very disappointing plants and flowers. I was expecting tulips the size of elephants and miles of brightly coloured petals. It was not to be, there was a fine mist coming down and the place just looked dreary and forlorn, lots of off-white tents selling tat.

15: Eurohash 2005 Amsterdam

We didn't stay long, and as we walked down the road we met some members of the UK Vecta Night Hash They invited us to go and get a coffee and some cake. *Unfortunate person* reckoned he could get some special hash cake from a place down the road. We went into a bar down a back ally and they purchased some cake, it came with the following instructions.

Hash cake is not like smoking hashish; it is a completely different effect. If you have not tried it before you should taste a small corner of a piece then wait for at least an hour to see how it affects you

By the time I had read the bit about only eating a quarter of a slice *Heinz* had consumed a small loaf. Everyone else from the night hash had just a little nibble The Isle of Wighters had beer, except those unfortunates like me who had to drive. I enjoyed my coffee and we then had a discussion on what to do next. We quickly decided that it was not a day for outdoor pursuits so we headed for the Sex Museum.

This is on the main Damrack just down from the station. We paid our two euros and went inside. It had lots of historical pictures very tastefully displayed on the first floor. There was also a reconstruction of a back alley where prostitutes sold their wares (so to speak). It reminded me of the area around our hotel. An animatronics model of a gross woman moved towards you with arms open wide and sprayed water. There were pendants, black and white photographs and films, all with a sexual theme. Pottery models of Roman gods with huge willies, half man half beast three quarters penis!

There was lots of historical information about pornography through the ages - how censorship changes with time and culture. On the first floor was a collection of display stands with various sex aids displayed. There was an old 'what the butler saw' machine and several huge penises made into the shape of chairs. You could sit on a giant penis and have your photograph taken. Several of us did: we thought they would make good postcards. *Heinz* was by this time feeling the effects of the space cake; she was floating around laughing at the well-hung exhibits. She went to visit the loo and was convinced it was talking to her. (We found out later it was, when it is flushed a voice says 'Now wash your hands!')

There were historical books and magazines on the top floor with telephone booths to try some phone sex. In fact any method of distributing information seems to have been used by pornographers.

This is probably not really surprising - sex is one of the strongest urges among humans. About 80% of all Internet searches are sex related: four out of five web sites on the entire web are about pornography. I know being British we really should not be interested in sex (amazing there are any of us left) in fact we have for years had one of the highest levels of censorship of any European nation. Things are becoming a little more liberal in Britain today but compared to Holland we are still in a nanny state.

On the way out we got a phone call from Cooperman and Snowman. They wanted to know when we were getting back to the hotel so we could move on to the castle and set our tents up. We went out into a sheet of solid water! This was serious rain. After buying some umbrellas from a local shop we hurried back to our hotel. Well, we waited for an hour and eventually a soggy Coops and Snowman appeared; they had decided to wait in the bar until the rain stopped. Of course it never stopped so they were just delaying the inevitable and getting drunk (a fairly good plan really).

After spending another half an hour trying to convince Coops it was a good idea to make our way to the station, Snowman and I started out by ourselves and told him we would meet him at the castle. We rushed up to the platform and got on our train as it was leaving. Again we tried to pay but were not allowed to. At last we were on our way. As we relaxed on our journey through the suburbs of Amsterdam Snowman's phone went - it was Cooperman asking 'where are you, you bastards why did you leave me behind?' I left Snowman to use his tact and explain to Coops that we had waited quite a long time for him. He was on the train behind us and would meet us at Heemskirk station where I hoped to find my car in one piece.

Arriving at Heemskirk with fingers crossed I saw the Rover through the window, still with four wheels and windows. We waited for Cooperman to arrive on the train behind us. It turned up with no sign of Cooperman. We waited for the next one, still no Coops. Snowman phoned him and he said we were going to the castle to register and he could catch the shuttle bus with the big crowd who were waiting at the station.

The castle is now a hostel for backpackers. It is most impressive from the outside. Apparently the oldest part of the castle dates back to the 13th century. The inside has been restored in the original style but with modern facilities. It is also reported to have a ghost: a woman

15: Eurohash 2005 Amsterdam

who was forced to drink herself to death. Some of the hash seem quite happy to drink themselves to death. They certainly do not need forcing!

It was a very impressive looking building made of brick with turrets and a large bridge across a moat. Inside there was a queue of hashers trying to register; Snowman and I were behind the Guernsey girls who were being girly and excited. We got half way down the queue and who contacted us on his mobile but Cooperman. 'Can you pick me up from the station?' he asked. 'I will have to register first as I am halfway down the registration queue' I said.

We registered and went outside where there were several Vikings drinking beer out of their horns and making lots of noise. Round the corner appeared Cooperman who could not be bothered to wait for us and got a taxi. It was of course our fault entirely that he had to spend money. I just knew we were not going to hear the last of this for a long time to come.

We erected our tents next to Higgins and Sex Goddess. Sex Goddess is a small balding bloke with glasses. Apparently, when he was named there was a stunning Harriet (female hasher) who was being named at the same time. She was desperate to get the name Sex Goddess so naturally the GM gave it to him instead.

We sat out by our tents; watched the sun go down, drank a few beers and listened to Cooperman moaning about spending money on a taxi. We wandered inside for the evening meal: this was chilli con carne with rice and Cooperman moaning, as a side dish.

The evening run was a moonlit pub-crawl around Heemskirk, the only problems being that there was no moon and there are virtually no pubs to crawl around. We ran round miles of streets and occasionally had a beer stop at a van that followed us. The only pub I spotted was so full they wouldn't even let any more locals in - three hundred hashers had no chance! It was a long, dark and boring run around desolate streets; no moon, no hills and no countryside to run through. The best way to have a good night out in Heemskirk is to go to Amsterdam!

We returned to the castle, tired from running but virtually sober. I fell into my tent and went to sleep.

The next morning was the medieval tournament. There were tug of war contests and Jousting on a Bike with a cardboard horse's head on the front and a tail on the back. The object was to use a lance to collect rings from high up spots around a circular course without stopping the bike. It was impossible. I managed to make the horse go lame by breaking the bicycle chain.

I was better at staff fighting. These were made of wood padded with plastic foam. The aim was to get your opponent to step out of a circular area by hitting them with the staff. It is dead easy if your opponent is smaller and lighter than you. I chose my opponents carefully!

We collected our packed lunches and headed for the buses. A few of the Isle of Wighters had chosen the Flower Festival run. This was in a park by Amsterdam airport built, a few years ago, for an international flower festival. It was a well-landscaped park with a huge lake in the middle. There was even a waterfall. The water was pumped over the top of the Visitors' Centre and came down between glass panels, so you could walk through the cascading water, if you so desired. This is probably the only waterfall in Holland, as it is not renowned for its hills.

We ran around the whole of the park, jogging through woods and past some beautiful flora. We then went jumping across stepping-stones or, in some cases, falling off stepping-stones. Mongrel frolicked in the water for a while then went off to fetch a stick.

It was all very pleasant and we returned to the coach for down downs in high spirits. The down downs were in tins and most of the offences were to do with water: falling off stepping stones; getting soaked in waterfalls; urinating on the boys' side of the bush (don't ask); basically all sophisticated stuff!

The buses took us back to the castle where we showered and returned to the tents for a snooze. When we awoke Cooperman had appeared and he told us about the flattest ball breaker he had ever been on. It made up in distance what it lacked in height. He then moaned about paying for his taxi the day before and went in search of beer. He brought us a tray of beers over and we enjoyed drinking them, while chatting to Sex Goddess and Higgins. Higgins had an anatomically correct rubber chicken in his tent. I did not ask why.

15: Eurohash 2005 Amsterdam

Evening meal was baked potato and salad, and then it was time for some entertainment. There was an apple-bobbing contest where apples were bobbed from a paddling pool, boys versus girls. As each round was completed, clothes where removed until it became a wet T-shirt and underwear contest. Fairly entertaining, but I never worked out who won.

A group of the girls had a musical dance routine that involved them dancing in towels with very little underneath. They would then open their towels and flash at different points in the routine, making sure that no one could see anything. All I can say is that it didn't go completely to plan, particularly the bit about the audience not seeing anything.

It was then time to get ready for the fancy dress party - medieval theme of course. There were lots of ladies in flowing gowns; Gisbert was dressed as a court jester. I was dressed as a knight and had loads of fun guarding the drawbridge. I would stand stock still as though made of wax, wait until someone who looked nervous approached, then leap in front of them with my sword at their throat. I would ask for a password or a kiss to pass, depending on their sex.

It then started to rain again and everyone had to move inside. The disco was fun but the outdoor bar was soaked. There was thunder and lightning in the sky as a fire-eater entertained us all. God knows how they do it without burning their mouths.

The music was good, 70s and 80s stuff, and we all bopped the night away. I returned to a tent that had been converted into a swimming pool; it was soaking in the outer tent with one or two dry patches in the inner one. I found a relatively dry spot and fell into a coma until 11am the next day.

A Cooperman, who was moaning about taxis and wanted to go on the hangover run, awoke me. I said I didn't feel up to it and neither did Snowman but we offered to pick him up after the run if he got the bus out. As it was he didn't get his tent down in time, so we ended up starting the journey home about 2pm. It turned out that this was a good thing. We made good time through Holland and used warp drive through Belgium. It was about 5pm when we arrived in France. However, we tried everywhere and all the towns were full; no room at the camp sites or the hotels. What was going on I do not know! We even drove beyond Calais to Wissen and tried the hotels there -

nothing going. Eventually we found a lorry drivers' hotel in Calais, which was basic but had some rooms. We took them immediately.

It was now 8pm and all we wanted to do was relax. There was a bar at the hotel so we sampled the beer, then went in search of food. Cooperman asked the very pretty receptionist where the best seafood restaurant was. She told him it was right at the other end of town and gave him some directions.

Well, we walked for miles past hundreds of fantastic looking restaurants, Cooperman was determined to go to the one the receptionist had recommended. Snowman bet me that when Cooperman found the restaurant he would say it was too expensive and we would go back to one of the ones we had passed. Snowman must be clairvoyant because ten minutes later we were walking back the way we had come; it was getting late so we insisted that we all go into the first reasonable looking place we found.

We ended up in a restaurant called Fish and it was great; Cooperman and Snowman went for the moules again. I went for a platter of seafood including lobster, crab, whelks and numerous crustaceans with no name. I was given a toolbox to use with the meal, pliers, metal spikes, and knives with serrated edges. I spent two hours just trying to winkle the critters out of their shells. The price was very reasonable about fifteen pounds for the platter. I do not know why we cannot have restaurants like these in Britain, Dover is just twenty two miles across the water but the food over there is no comparison.

The next day we got up early and caught the ferry back to Blighty. A good crossing and an easy journey had us back on the Isle of Wight by 2pm. It is almost possible to go to Calais for lunch (there is a thought!) It was a great trip. Eurohash always is fantastic fun.

Eurohash 2009 will be in Turkey and Nash Hash 2009 will be in Scotland. Interhash 2008 is in Perth, Australia. If you would like to join the Drinking Club with the running problem, put WWW.Birminghamhash.co.uk into any search engine.

You won't regret it!

Navigator ON YOU!

Bibliography

Isle of Wight French T shirt by Mongrel

© Copyright
Mark. C. Williams
January 2006-2008

www.ingramcontent.com/pod-product-compliance
Lightning Source LLC
LaVergne TN
LVHW091308080426
835510LV00007B/407